Teach Now!
The Essentials of Teaching

The companion website for this series can be found at **www.routledge.com/cw/teachnow**. All of the useful web links highlighted in the book can be found here, along with additional resources and activities.

Being taught by a great teacher is one of the genuine privileges of life. Teach Now! *is an exciting new series that opens up the secrets of great teachers and, step by step, helps trainees and new recruits to the profession to build the skills and confidence they need to become first-rate classroom practitioners.*

Teach Now! The Essentials of Teaching provides the fundamental knowledge for becoming a great teacher. Combining a grounded, modern rationale for learning and teaching with highly practical training approaches, it covers everything you need to know, from preparing for teaching practice to getting your first job.

Harnessing a range of simple, but powerful, techniques, the book shows you how you can translate the Teachers' Standards into your own classroom practice and provide the evidence that you have met them. It also demystifies what the best teachers know and do instinctively to create students who want to learn and get a buzz from developing new skills. The book is structured in clear parts that are then divided into short, easy-to-absorb units offering clear, straightforward advice on all aspects of teaching including:

- why teach?;
- the application and recruitment process for training;
- helping students achieve good progress;

- planning, differentiation and assessment;
- behaviour management;
- using language effectively in the classroom;
- managing parents' evenings;
- being an effective tutor;
- how to have lunch!

With talking points to encourage reflection and a wide range of examples to illustrate practice, *Teach Now! The Essentials of Teaching* provides expert guidance as you start your exciting and rewarding career as an outstanding teacher.

Geoff Barton is Headteacher of King Edward VI School, a large state comprehensive school in Suffolk, UK. He has written and edited more than 100 books on English and school leadership. He is a Founding Fellow of the English Association and a regular writer and speaker on education.

Teach Now!

Series editor: Geoff Barton

Being taught by a great teacher is one of the genuine privileges of life. *Teach Now!* is an exciting new series that opens up the secrets of great teachers and, step by step, helps trainees and new recruits to the profession to build the skills and confidence they need to become first-rate classroom practitioners. The series comprises a core text that explores what every teacher needs to know about essential issues, such as learning, pedagogy, assessment and behaviour management, and subject-specific books that guide the reader through the key components and challenges in teaching individual subjects. Written by expert practitioners, the books in this series combine an underpinning philosophy of teaching and learning alongside engaging activities, strategies and techniques to ensure success in the classroom.

Titles in the series:

Teach Now!
The Essentials of Teaching

What You Need to Know
to Be a Great Teacher

Geoff Barton

Routledge
Taylor & Francis Group

LONDON AND NEW YORK

First published 2015
by Routledge
2 Park Square, Milton Park, Abingdon, Oxon OX14 4RN

and by Routledge
711 Third Avenue, New York, NY 10017

Routledge is an imprint of the Taylor & Francis Group, an informa business

© 2015 Geoff Barton

The right of Geoff Barton to be identified as author of this work has been asserted by him in accordance with sections 77 and 78 of the Copyright, Designs and Patents Act 1988.

Trademark notice: Product or corporate names may be trademarks or registered trademarks, and are used only for identification and explanation without intent to infringe.

British Library Cataloguing in Publication Data
A catalogue record for this book is available from the British Library

Library of Congress Cataloging in Publication Data
Barton, Geoff.
Teach now! the essentials of teaching: what you need to know to be a great teacher/Geoff Barton.
pages cm – (Teach now!)
1 (ebook) 1. Teaching. 2. Teachers – Training of. I. Title.
LB1025.3.B365 2014
371.102 – dc23
2014019075

ISBN: 978-0-415-71490-7 (hbk)
ISBN: 978-0-415-71491-4 (pbk)
ISBN: 978-1-315-74484-1 (ebk)

Typeset in Celeste and Optima
by Florence Production Ltd, Stoodleigh, Devon, UK

Contents

Contents

Contents

Contents

Series editor's foreword

What is this series about, and who is it for?

Many of us unashamedly like being teachers.

We shrug off the jibes about being in it for the holidays. We ignore the stereotypes in soap operas, sitcoms, bad films and serious news programmes. We don't feel any need to apologise for what we do, despite a constant and corrosive sense of being undervalued.

We always knew that being criticised was part of the deal.

We aren't defensive. We aren't apologetic. We simply like teaching.

And whether we still spend the majority of our working week teaching classes or, as senior leaders, we regard the classroom as a sanctuary from the swirling madness beyond the school gates, we think teaching matters.

In fact, we think it matters a lot.

And we think that students need more good teachers.

That's where *Teach Now!* started as a concept. Could we – a group of teachers and teaching leaders, scattered across England – put together the kind of books that we wished we had had when we were embarking on our own journeys into the secret garden of education?

Of course, there were lots of books around then. Nowadays, there are even more – books, plus ebooks, blogs and tweets. You can hardly move on the Internet without tripping over another reflection on a lesson that went well or badly, or another teacher extolling a particular approach or dismissing another craze or moaning about the management.

So we know you don't necessarily think you need us. There are plenty of people out there ready to shovel advice and guidance towards a fledgling teacher.

But we wanted to do something different. We wanted to provide two essential texts that would distil our collective knowledge as teachers and package it in a form that was easy to read, authoritative, re-readable, reassuring and deeply rooted in the day-to-day realities of education as it is – not as a consultant or adviser might depict it.

We are writing, in other words, in the early hours of days when each of us will be teaching classes, taking assemblies, watching lessons, looking at schemes of work and dealing with naughty students – and possibly naughty teachers.

We believe this gives our series a distinctive sense of being grounded in the routines of real schools, the kind of places we each work in every day.

We want to provide a warts-and-all account of how to be a great teacher, but we also each believe that education is an essentially optimistic career.

However grim the news out there, in our classrooms we can weave a kind of magic, given the right conditions and the right behaviour. We can reassure ourselves and the students in front of us that, together, we can make the world better.

And, if that seems far-fetched, then you haven't seen enough great teachers.

As Roy Blatchford – himself an exceptional teacher and now the Director of the National Education Trust – says in his list of what great teachers do:

The best teachers are children at heart
Sitting in the best lessons, you just don't want to leave.
(Roy Blatchford, *The 2012 Teachers' Standards in the Classroom*, Sage, 2013)

We want young people to experience more lessons like that – classrooms where the sense of time is different, where it expands and shrinks, as the world beyond the classroom recedes, and where interest and passion and fascination take over; places where, whatever your background, your brain will fire with new experiences, thoughts and ideas; where, whatever your experience so far of the adult world, here, in this classroom, is an adult who cares a lot about something, can communicate it vividly and, in the way she or he talks and behaves, demonstrates care and seemingly endless interest in you.

We need more classrooms like that and more teachers to take their place within them.

So that's what we have set out to do: to create a small series of books that will, if you share our sense of moral purpose, help you to become a great teacher. We have used our experience, plus 'official' documents such as the national Teachers' Standards, to write something that we hope you find eminently practical, as well as being underpinned by genuine pedagogical principles.

Thus you'll have a text that will help you to understand how to translate the Teachers' Standards into your own really strong classroom practice. We will show you how to provide the evidence that you have met those Standards. This will be essential as you develop into a confident teacher looking for career progression.

But we want to do much more than that – to show you the things great teachers do that aren't so easily reduced to a government checklist and that will result in real teaching that creates students who love knowledge and get a buzz from developing new skills.

You'll have noticed that, if you are intending to teach English, History, Mathematics, Modern Foreign Languages or Science, then we expect you to buy two books, because we think that being a great teacher has two important dimensions to it.

First, you need to know your subject – to *really* know it. We know from very good sources that the most effective teachers are experts in what they teach. That doesn't mean they know everything about it. In fact, they often fret about how little they feel they truly know.

But they are hungry and passionate and eager – and all those other characteristics that define the teachers who inspire us.

So we know that subject knowledge is really important – and not just for teaching older students. It is as important when teaching Year 7s, knowing what you need to teach and what you can, for now, ignore.

We also believe that subject knowledge is much more than a superficial whisk through key dates or key concepts. It's about having a depth of understanding that allows us to join up ideas, to explore complexity and nuance, to make decisions about what the key building-blocks of learning a subject might be.

Great teachers sense this and, over a number of years, they build their experience and hone their skills. That's why we have developed subject specialist books for English, Mathematics, History, Modern Foreign Languages and Science. These are the books that will help you to take what you learned on your degree course and to think through how to make that knowledge and those skills powerfully effective in the classroom.

They will take you from theory to practice, from philosophy into pedagogy. They will help to show you that any terror you may have about becoming a teacher of a subject is inevitable and that knowing your stuff, careful planning, informed strategies – all of these will help you to teach now.

Then there's this book. This is your core text, because we also believe that, even if you are the best-informed scientist, linguist or mathematician in the universe, this in itself won't make you a great teacher.

That's because great teachers do things that support and supplement their subject knowledge. This is the stuff that the late great educator Michael Marland called the 'craft of the classroom'. It's what the best teachers know and do instinctively, but, to those of us looking on from the outside, or from the earliest stages of a teaching career, can seem mysterious, unattainable, a kind of magic.

It's also the kind of stuff that conventional training may not sufficiently cover.

We're talking about how to open the classroom door, knowing where to stand, knowing what to say to the student who is cheeky, knowing how to survive when you feel, in the darkest of glooms, intimidated by more late-night preparation and by relentless marking, that you have made a terrible career choice.

These two texts combined – the subject specialist book and the core book – are designed to help you wherever you are training – in a school or academy or on a PGCE course. Whether you are receiving expert guidance, or it's proving to be more mixed, we hope our ideas, approaches and advice will reassure you and help you to gain in confidence.

We hope we are providing books that you will want to read and re-read as you train, as you take up your first post and as you finally shrug off the feelings of early insecurity and start to stretch your wings as a fully fledged teacher.

So that's the idea behind the books.

And, throughout the writing of them, we have been very conscious that – just like us – you have too little time. We have therefore aimed to write in a style that is easy to read, reassuring, occasionally provocative and opinionated. We don't want to be bland: teaching is too important for any of us to wilt under a weight of colourless eduspeak.

That's why we have written in short paragraphs, short chapters, added occasional points for reflection and discussion, comments from trainee and veteran teachers, and aimed throughout to create practical, working guides to help you teach now.

So, thanks for choosing to read what we have written. We would love to hear how your early journey into teaching goes and hope that our series helps you successfully navigate your way into and through a brilliant and rewarding career in teaching.

Geoff Barton
with Sally Allan, Mike Gershon, Alex Quigley,
Tom Sherrington and Julia Upton
The *Teach Now!* team of authors

Who are you?

Hello. Here's who I think you are.

I'm imagining you as someone who may have toyed with the idea of becoming a teacher, but may have worried about whether it is the right career choice.

You may have been told by people that you'd make a great teacher, but you aren't so sure. You aren't yet convinced about the public perception or the workload or the salary or the status or the whole business of managing the behaviour of young people who are so often depicted in the media as wayward, feckless and out of control.

Or you may have known teachers and – to be frank – thought, 'I don't want to end up like them'.

Or you may have worried that you weren't cut out for a job that gets so much bad press, carries with it so many expectations, and that can appear, from the outside, to have so few perks beyond the quota of holidays.

So – truth be told – I'm not writing this for the reader who knew at the age of four that teaching was the career path for them. If that does describe you, then you are, of course, more than welcome to read on, and even more welcome to buy lots of copies of this book for friends and family. In fact, I would recommend doing so.

But it is the wavering, insecure and decidedly undecided reader that I'm most interested in.

Why?

Because that was what I was like, many years ago.

And because you're just the kind of person I believe teaching needs.

It sometimes seems as if there aren't enough really great teachers to go round. We need more people who feel a mission to join us in education, to help us to prepare young people to take on a world that is likely to be far more complicated and challenging than it was when we left school.

We need to give them the skills and knowledge, but also, crucially, the attitudes, resilience and leadership, which will help their generation to make a better job of improving the world than my generation has.

We need teachers who sense the urgency of this, who are relentless in their wish to be outstanding teachers and who, in turn, create outstanding learners.

And we need to do this against a backdrop where teachers endure constant verbal sniping, where we are seen as people who can 'talk but can't do', and where too many politicians think it's their right to meddle endlessly in what happens in the classroom.

So yes: we need a generation of teachers to add to the great teachers already working in our schools. And we need you now.

In my experience, there are two kinds of brilliant teacher – those who have always known they want to teach, who somehow have an intuitive ability. That wasn't me. And then there are those who are cautiously interested but also nervous. Often, they have flirted with other careers. Then they make for teaching, learn the craft and are superb.

That, I think, is who you are. And – I would like to think – it's who I am too.

TALKING POINTS

- Which teacher has had the biggest effect on you – either for positive or negative reasons?
- Which teacher from your own schooldays would you most like to emulate? Why?

Who am I?

I'm writing this on the day of my fifty-first birthday. Something happens as you get older. You get more accustomed to the seasons; you appreciate them more. You become nostalgic about decisions made many years ago and where they have led you. And you become increasingly conscious that life is finite, that time runs out.

A birthday is a particular day for doing that.

So today, writing this, I think of what I had wanted to do when I was at school.

My brother had been to the local grammar school. This was the cusp of comprehensive education in England, and so I escaped the 11+ examination and went to the shiny local comprehensive school.

My mother, it has to be said, never quite approved of it. It was called Walton Comprehensive, and I think it was the initials 'WC' that made her think it somehow wasn't good enough. But it served me well, in particular because I was taught on two occasions by an exceptional English teacher.

Mr Samson taught me when I was a young and nervy Year 7 pupil and then again when – after scraping a clutch of decidedly mediocre O levels and trying to leave the school to become the next Radio 1 breakfast DJ (I failed) – I landed in the sixth form.

Until this point, teaching was the last job I would have considered, a perception exacerbated by the fact that it had, in those days, an exceptionally low status.

Who am I?

But Mr Samson, like so many inspiring teachers, wove a kind of magic. He did what I've since seen hundreds of great teachers do: he took the complicated and rendered it not just simpler, but also compelling.

Shakespeare, I realised, was someone I just had to know more about. Obscure eighteenth-century poems were suddenly unmissable. Novels that I thought too off-puttingly thick even to start were made manageable by skilful teaching, coaxing and feedback.

Yes, suddenly I too wanted to be a teacher. Or, more specifically, I wanted to be Mr Samson.

So that's what I set about doing. I achieved a decidedly mixed set of A levels, headed to read English at Lancaster University, found that I loved my subject even more than I had expected and then transplanted myself to Leicester University for a PGCE course.

I found not only that I could teach (though not brilliantly), but also that I liked teaching, and it's what I've been doing since.

And even though these days my day job is as headteacher of a large and proudly comprehensive secondary school in Suffolk, I would find it unthinkable if it didn't consist of me actually teaching.

So, that's what I do – this year teaching English to two A level groups, two Year 11 and Year 10 classes.

Through the years, I have spent a lot of time teaching and watching hundreds of teachers – many brilliant, some terrible – and from the process, I have learned more about how to become a better teacher. I've probably learned as much from watching bad teachers as from watching the superstars.

I don't write this book from any sense that I'm a brilliant teacher. I know that I'm not. But I remain hungry to improve endlessly and passionate about helping other teachers – whether new to the profession or seasoned veterans – to keep improving too.

So, that's me.

I hope this gives you some context for the 'voice' at the heart of this book, because I am determinedly not dishing up a lucky bag of 'tips for teachers'.

Instead, I want to provide you with the kind of book I wish I had had when I started – written by someone who has been around for a while, has worked in 'real' schools with 'real' students in various towns and cities, and who knows that, even after almost thirty years in the job, you can have very bad days, as well as very good ones.

This book is my attempt to help you to become a highly effective, motivating and reflective teacher, and to do so pretty quickly.

I hope you enjoy it.

TALKING POINTS

- How similar was your experience of school to mine?
- If you were setting up a school from scratch, what might be its three essential ingredients?

How to read this book

That, I suspect, will seem like one of the more bizarre chapter headings of this book, but I think it's worth spelling out how I'm envisaging that you might read this.

I'm guessing that, although you might start by reading it through, you will probably get to points that won't seem relevant yet – they are the bits on the more technical aspects of teaching, the important stuff about how to stand, how to explain things, how to develop your students into more independent thinkers, and so on.

I'm guessing that there are some bits that you will want to read before your training starts, perhaps before you have applied for training, and then other bits that you will want to read and re-read when you're in the thick of teaching practice.

That's how I'm imagining the book will work – and that one day it will strike you as old hat, redundant, full of now-obvious reflections, patronizing. You will have made it as an effective teacher and will have no need of the text again and, like that box of toys in *Toy Story 3*, I'll be consigned to a box under the bed, a cupboard or jumble sale. In that case, I'm hoping that it will be mission accomplished – that you will have gained what you wanted from the text: a mix of reassurance, philosophy, principles and real, hard-nosed, practical advice.

However, there is one other suggestion I want to make about how you read. I urge you to read actively. By that I mean underline bits, put asterisks, turn down pages – and make notes.

Despite all the work you're going to have during your training, especially as you start to teach more lessons, I recommend that you keep a diary or journal. I explicitly don't say a blog: I'm not suggesting you write some public version of your experiences – that sense of an audience would be bound to change what you say.

As you are training to teach, navigating your way through the highs and lows, you need mental space to pause and reflect and reconsider.

I'd suggest that the combination of this book, the subject-specific book and a diary, notebook or word-processing file – all these will help to make your development as a teacher richer, that the discipline of writing a few lines a day – a paragraph, a thought, a feeling – will make you a more reflective teacher. And you will look back on what you write one day with a fascinating, sometimes poignant, sometimes embarrassing, sense of who you – your younger self – were and what you have learned in the interim.

So that is how I would recommend you read this book – which is to say, how you embark on becoming a teacher.

TALKING POINTS

- So, are you going to do that – keep some kind of reflective journal?
- If so, how, and where?

Part I

Before training to teach

Taking the decision to become a teacher is a big step. Some of us knew at school, when we were taught by a great teacher, that this was something we wanted to do.

Others – based perhaps on a succession of mediocre teachers – decided it was most definitely not the career for us.

And yet, and yet . . . there's something about the career of teaching that just won't leave the headlines, won't stop gnawing at our consciousness, whether for good or bad reasons.

A good friend of mine, Ian Gilbert, wrote a book called *Why Do I Need a Teacher When I've Got Google?*. It's a great title and a great book.

But the reality is that we do need teachers. We need great teachers – and we need more of them.

So this short section is designed to help you in deciding whether you're definitely going to embark on a new career trajectory into teaching, and, if so, what route you'll take into this noble, but often misrepresented, profession.

Hold on tight: your career as a teacher is about to begin.

1

How to know whether teaching is the career for you

Teaching doesn't always get the best media coverage. Those working in education can often feel that they are unappreciated and unloved, or that the demanding nature of the job is frequently misrepresented in the media and by politicians. We feel that too many social issues – from youth unemployment, through obesity and antisocial behaviour, to a shortage of computer programmers – are blamed on our shortcomings. If only we taught better, the narrative seems to run, then all would be well.

As a result, teachers can often seem prickly and defensive.

Those outside the profession view the regular news stories about how we are sliding down the international league tables or how state schools are little more than unruly menageries in which hapless teachers attempt, ineffectively, to contain the riotous hordes and can't be blamed for thinking that, at the core of any problems our society might have, is a set of feckless teachers.

In reality, of course, there are good schools and poor schools and, within each, good teachers and poor teachers – just as there will be good and poor solicitors, doctors, mechanics, lawyers and politicians.

So, if you want to become a teacher, it's worth detaching yourself from lots of the stereotypes. Instead, flick through this book. Look at what teachers say about the job. I asked a hundred of them to tell me what they think of the job. Some are at the start of their careers. Some are gnarly veterans. Some specialise at Key Stage 3 (KS3); others teach mostly A level students. All are real teachers, doing the job day in and day out.

Read their comments and see how you react: whether they draw you in and attract you to teaching as a career, or whether they put you off.

I asked them to write down:

- what they like about the job;
- what frustrates them;
- what one piece of advice they would give to someone embarking on teaching as a career.

Their comments are distributed across the pages of this book. I was struck by their candour and freshness.

Your first impression of the comments of practising teachers may give you a stronger insight into why you are thinking of teaching and whether it's the right career for you.

TALKING POINTS

- Which of these comments are most attractive to you?
- Which speak to you most?
- Do any put you off?
- Do any surprise you?
- If you had to give your two main impulses for becoming a teacher, what would they be?

2 So, what are you worrying about?

Everyone worries before they embark on a new career.

Teaching, however, appears to carry with it distinctive terrors, because it's not just about whether you have the skills and knowledge to do the job; it's knowing also that you're going to be judged every lesson, every day, by that most discerning group of judges – the students you finally teach.

That adds a certain frisson to the worry many would-be teachers feel before they embark on their training, before they teach a lesson, before the start of a new term or, indeed, week, because one of the little-known realities of teaching is that we are all prone to worry. Too often, of course, we are presented in the media as complacent idlers who are only in it for the holidays. Or, at least, during our neurotic low points, that's how it can feel.

I know from experience that a very striking feature of the psychological landscape of many teachers is that worry never goes away. It hits its peak on Sunday evenings and during the elongated final hours of any holiday.

Even those of us who are veterans of many classrooms, in many schools, over many years, still get this – and it invades our dreams. It's the worry that we won't be able to control a class, or that they will laugh at us, or that we will show we don't know or can't do what we thought we could.

Before training to teach

This is the dark, inner world of the teacher's mind, and you might as well know now that, just as the best actors continue to undergo sometimes crippling degrees of stage fright, so even the greatest teachers worry about how a lesson will go. Sometimes that worry is deep and unshakable.

With this in mind, I asked a group of PGCE trainees to make a list of the questions and concerns they had at the start of their training. This was in the early days of their training. I asked a group of School Direct trainees to do the same.

The result is a set of questions that I'm going to use to frame this book. Here's what those about to step into teaching are worrying about.

At the end of the book (on p. 191), I'll return to them, go through them and make sure each one has been addressed.

For now, read them through and see which ones especially capture how you might be feeling.

1 What happens if I walk into a classroom and they all laugh at me?

2 Is there a good way to increase my confidence?

3 Are there any good ways of learning names?

4 What are the best things to write in my personal statement before applying?

5 What is the best way to design a worksheet?

6 How do I write a lesson plan?

7 How open can I be with students about my own belief (religious or political)?

8 What happens if I don't have a pigeonhole?

9 Will there be coffee on tap?

10 What should I wear on my first day?

11 What do I do if a student tells me something personal about their background – e.g. that they are being abused?

TALKING POINTS

- Which three questions are most relevant to what you are feeling?
- Which three are least relevant?
- What questions of your own would you add?

WHAT I LOVE ABOUT TEACHING

The kids! They make your day when they say great things about your lesson/when they have pride in what they've accomplished/when they say something funny/random and it makes you smile.

3 How important is training to be a teacher?

Teaching needs talented people.

For too many years – by which I mean centuries, in fact – our experience as pupils has too often depended on the lottery of which teacher we happened to have for a particular subject.

Many of us found that we enjoyed and were good at a subject because, for the first time, a certain teacher brought it alive. Many of us chose courses in that subject as a result. I specialised in English because I happened to have an English teacher who inspired me, who made me realise that I could do this subject and who planted in my mind the thought that I too might like to study English at a higher level and then teach it.

Imagine if, instead, we had been taught by someone clueless or hapless or hopeless or dull.

Most of them will have trained as teachers. So, if such people can be unleashed in our classrooms and achieve qualified teacher status (QTS), then is it worth training teachers? Aren't the best teachers born, not made?

From time to time, there are debates about whether really good teachers need to be trained or not, whether they need formal qualifications.

I read one such article this morning, by leading educationist and headmaster of Wellington College in Berkshire, Anthony Seldon. Writing in *The Guardian*, he says:

Before training to teach

The teacher's role is much more akin to that of a parent. It is a great loss that governments worldwide have made teaching much less like being a parent than an impersonal civil servant. No job is more important than parenting, yet no one is suggesting parents go off for a university course to qualify as a parent. Parents pick it up as they go along, and that's exactly the way great teachers are forged.

There is one fundamental difference between parenting and teaching. The former are self-selecting, whereas the latter have to be appointed by those with knowledge and experience. I write this from a conference on Education for Tomorrow run by Singapore Management University. The principals attending are from schools around the world, state and private, and almost all agree that great teaching is a gift that some have, and others will never acquire even if they spend 10 years locked away in a university. Most of us can tell within minutes whether someone has 'got it' or not.

(Anthony Seldon, 'Teaching is like parenting: you don't need to have a qualification', *The Guardian*, 28 October 2013)

What do you make of this? If you are about to embark on training as a teacher, how do you respond to the message that being a teacher is akin to a branch of parenting, that the need to learn the craft has been overstated?

Is the analogy actually correct – is the teacher's role similar to what might be expected of a parent? And, if it is, aren't there in fact some parents who definitely would benefit from undergoing some training?

Think of the really talented teachers who have influenced you: was it the case that you could tell within minutes that they 'had it', or were their skills subtler and less obvious?

Certainly, my thirty years have shown me that, although there are some instinctive teachers – people who can walk into a classroom and teach with authority and skill – most of us benefit from a training programme that combines some element of theory with lots of observation of other teachers and the chance to practise the skills you are developing.

The best teachers will continue to see themselves as learning throughout their careers and, although they will know that certain parts of the job will become effortless and unconscious, they are also likely to get nervous before results day, to worry about whether certain groups are doing well enough and to reflect endlessly on how they might teach a topic better.

This, in reality, is what great teachers do – training isn't an irrelevance, an afterthought, an optional extra. A certificate proving that you have undergone a professional programme of tuition isn't something we should downplay, any more than we would want to employ a solicitor who hasn't studied law or a dentist who hasn't been to dental school.

Training, you will find, is fundamental to the job of a teacher, a core part of the mission to become better at explaining, at assessing, at helping students to learn.

TALKING POINTS

- What do you agree with in Anthony Seldon's article? In your experience, are great teachers like parents?
- Can you tell within minutes whether someone has 'got it' or not? If so, what exactly is the 'it', and what are the telltale signs of someone who can teach well?
- What are the arguments for and against teachers having a teaching qualification?

4 How do admissions tutors view prospective applicants for teacher training?

Specifically for this book, I talked to an admissions tutor at one of the UK's top PGCE providers – a university-based teacher training course. I asked her for her insights on the recruitment process: what is she looking for in prospective teachers?

Here's what she said:

> I imagine that the students thinking of applying for a PGCE place would value the same kind of advice as those applying for other routes.
>
> Their application needs to convince its readers that they are committed to becoming a teacher (they will have spent time with children of the age they intend to teach, they will have enjoyed working with them, they will have a good idea about what life in a school is like, they will have considered why they want to teach and why they want to teach the subject that they have applied for).
>
> They will probably have considered what it is about them that makes them likely to be a good teacher, and why they think they will find teaching personally satisfying and enriching.
>
> It doesn't need purple prose and it doesn't need to be full of jargon, but it does need to show a genuine interest in their becoming teachers. Some students tell mini-stories to illustrate a point. Some students explain what it is about a PGCE that

attracts them as one way of showing that they have thought carefully about being a teacher and what route might suit them best. Their feelings about their subject and how it contributes to an education also tend to come across.

But I don't think that there are any golden rules.

The fact that they have (or haven't) done some lesson observations or perhaps taken some responsibility in their communities will be revealing (but they don't have to be BANG! WHAM! ACTION! 'I-ARRANGED-A-SPONSORED-SWIM-ACROSS-THE-CHANNEL-AND-THEN-TREKKED-ACROSS-THE-SAHARA' super heroes – all kinds of people can be excellent teachers).

The fact that they do/do not have coherent reasons for becoming a teacher (and probably of this particular subject) will similarly speak volumes. During the course and during their careers their views and opinions will develop. They aren't expected, before they start, to have it all sewn up – but they are expected to be thoughtful.

This will get them an interview (so long as there are still places on the course – they can apply at various points in the year but courses get filled up).

When they are interviewed the interviewer will check whether the impression given on the application form is correct – this person does really want to teach and has done enough before the course to know what teaching might involve (so that school life doesn't turn out to be a complete shock).

Also important: will they be teachable? Do they show the capacity to think critically? How has their degree prepared them for the kind of specific subject knowledge that they will need (and, therefore, where there might be gaps, what might the candidate do to help gain the knowledge before the course starts).

TALKING POINTS

- What in this reassures you?
- What surprises you?
- How does it make you feel about your own suitability for a teaching course?

WHAT I DISLIKE ABOUT TEACHING

There's just not enough time to do everything. People outside the profession never believe that. They see only short days and holidays. But in reality I hate the feeling that I never have time to do anything really well.

5 How to secure a place on a teacher training course

The advice here is going to be short and pithy, and I have a feeling it will apply throughout the rest of your career as a teacher, any time you apply for a promotion or new role, in any institution.

It's this: a letter of application doesn't get you a training place or job or promotion. It gets you an interview.

So the aim shouldn't be for your letter and application form to encapsulate everything an interview panel will need to know about you. Much of that will come out from visiting the institution – the teacher training college, university or school – at interview, in your taught lesson and in your more informal interactions with staff there.

So the letter is important in one respect only: in getting you to your interview.

Use it to explain:

* why you want to be a teacher;
* what it is about teaching your subject specifically that attracts and excites you;
* what skills, qualities and experiences you bring to the job.

Some training providers may ask for different elements in your application. Some might, for example, ask you to write a reflection on a lesson you taught or a teacher who influenced you. They might ask you to bring this to discuss at interview.

Before training to teach

They might ask you to write a reflection (probably stipulating no more than 1,000 words) on some aspect of the existing curriculum in your subject. For example, one university-based PGCE provider sets a task like this:

> The National Curriculum is under review. Some schools are at liberty in any case to opt out of providing centrally prescribed curriculum content.
>
> On one side of A4, provide an outline of what your Geography curriculum would contain at Key Stage 3 (that is, Years 11–14) if you were designing it from scratch. Include the skills, knowledge and experiences you think should be made available to every student in that age group.
>
> Then, in a separate paper of no more than 1,000 words, write a reflection about your proposed curriculum. You will be asked to discuss your ideas as part of the interview process, either in a small group or in a one-to-one context.

Whatever you write should take exact account of what is being asked for. If they say 'no more than 1,000 words', write no more than that. As the task refers to 'skills, knowledge and experiences', you might use that framework to structure your submission.

Your A4 summary document might therefore look something like this:

Your commentary might be structured in exactly the same way as the outline, using the same subheadings, so that what you write in the reflective piece relates clearly and directly to the one-side outline of your curriculum.

Clarity like this counts for a lot. It's not only easier for the reader to follow, especially when reading quickly; it also says something about you and the way you work. It suggests to your audience that you are analytical, logical and precise and have the ability to make things reassuringly accessible. These are essential ingredients that most great teachers possess. You can demonstrate them in the way you ensure that your written submission directly matches what is being requested and makes it easy for your readers to find the information they require.

Name:

Key Stage 3 Geography: my proposals

Rationale: why Geography matters

[A brief paragraph stating the importance and relevance of Geography]

Skills:

[A paragraph or set of bullet points summarising the main skills that Geography can help students to develop]

Knowledge:

[Same again – this time for knowledge]

Experiences:

[Outline some of the experiences we might want students to have within our subject – such as field trips, conferences, visits, whole-day immersion in a specific topic: these are the kinds of experience that liberate our subject from the confines of the classroom, connecting it with the world beyond school.]

TALKING POINTS

- Start drafting what your key points will be for becoming a teacher (e.g. a sense of mission, enjoyment of working with young people, satisfaction of doing a job that can make a difference to others' futures).
- Note down why specifically you wish to teach your chosen subject – what is it about it that captures your

interest, why does it matter? What skills and qualities
does it help to develop?

- Begin to make some notes on the experiences you might
  want to include – activities that will demonstrate your
  ability to work patiently with others, to instruct, to be
  empathetic, to earn respect and so on.

ADVICE FOR NEW TEACHERS

Learn to use your time cleverly. If you find yourself waiting for ten minutes in the doctor's surgery, mark a couple of books. Seize time as best you can.

6 What to expect in the interview for a teacher training place

In the past, when gaining a teacher training place was perhaps less competitive, it may well have been the case that you would turn up for interview, be interviewed, leave and await a letter telling you whether you had been successful.

Now, the process is likely to be more systematic. You may be asked to bring something with you or to send it in advance – for example, the curriculum rationale referred to in Chapter 5. You may be expected to engage in a group discussion with other candidates who have been called for interview on the same day. Or you may be asked to have a discussion with a group of students.

The next chapter explores how to conduct yourself at interview, in order to optimise your chances of being successful. First though, consider the kinds of question you might be asked during an interview for a teacher training place:

- Question 1: How well do you think your earlier discussion session with other trainees/pupils went? How would you evaluate your contribution?

- Question 2: Why do you want to train as a teacher in your subject? What motivates you to work with young people?

- Question 3: What do you consider to be the qualities of a good teacher, and why do you think you will make a good teacher? Which teacher in your life has influenced you positively?

- Question 4: What experiences have you gained, and what skills have you developed in your previous work or roles that would be useful in teaching?

- Question 5: Tell us about something you think pupils would find challenging in your subject. Why would they find it challenging, and what could you do to help them overcome this difficulty?

- Questions 6 and 7: You might get some specific questions now about your subject – possibly based on a topic or concept that traditionally is perceived as difficult. A question might ask you to explain how you would present it in class to pupils to help them grasp the concept. Or you might be asked how you would teach a topic or concept to two different age groups, or two different ability groups. In the case of Modern Foreign Languages, expect to have to use the target language.

- Question 8: Imagine you are observing a lesson: how would you know that the lesson was going well? How would you judge whether pupils were learning what they were supposed to be learning?

- Question 9: If you were teaching a lesson and pupils' behaviour became disruptive, what strategies would you use to deal with the situation?

- Question 10: How would you seek to promote the moral, spiritual and cultural development of your pupils? What do you understand of the work of tutors in schools?

- Question 11: Your teacher training year will often be tough. You will work long hours, sometimes feel isolated and occasionally become very frustrated. What in your life has prepared you for dealing with pressure such as this? What coping mechanisms do you have?

- Question 12: Please read the list of conditions and disabilities on the card. In order for us to support you effectively as a trainee, please tell us which, if any, of the conditions listed apply to you. Is there anything we need to know about how we can best support you, if you are given a training place?

- Question 13: Is there anything you would like to ask us?

TALKING POINTS

- Are there any surprises in these questions?
- Which do you expect to find most straightforward? Which will be trickiest?
- Do you think it's necessary to have a question to ask (Question 13) of your interviewer?

WHAT I LOVE ABOUT TEACHING

Even though it sounds cheesy - you get to see that you are making a difference. Not always, of course, and perhaps not with every student, but definitely with some. It feels brilliant.

7 How to do well at interview for a training place

In recent years, there has been a relentless drive to get more of the best graduates into teaching. Despite the apparent complexity of ways into teaching, at the heart of the process will be an interview. This is where you will be able to demonstrate whether, crucially, you have the right temperament for teaching.

It's not a test to see whether you already exhibit the prototype qualities of a teacher. Any decent interview process will be based on knowing that teachers are made through practice and high-quality training. So you aren't expected to show that you are one of those 'born teachers'.

However, you will need to exemplify many of the essential traits that teachers of children of all ages, in schools of all types, need and demonstrate, day in and day out.

The interview process will be predicated on exploring these features of your personality, assessing how carefully you have reflected on the role and responsibilities of a teacher and whether you have the stamina, resilience and optimism for the role.

Remember that the trainers will be working to a checklist of the qualities and experience they are looking for in applicants and will be judging your letter of application and your performance during the interview against these criteria.

They are specifically looking for evidence, and so the more you can highlight examples of jobs, voluntary work and activities that match what they want, then the better you are likely to do.

You are likely to be interviewed by a panel of people – one perhaps from a university department (if applying for a PGCE course) and one a teacher in one of the partner schools of the department.

The questions won't be made up as the interviewers go along. They will have been mapped out in advance. There are some examples in the next section.

Bear in mind that interviewers will ask you a question and are likely to evaluate your answer using a scale such as this, grading each response based on the depth and understanding you display:

1 = there is very little evidence
2 = there is some evidence
3 = there is good evidence
4 = there is very good evidence

Although first impressions count for a lot – and you may charm the interviewers with your friendly manner and personable outlook – remember that they are likely to be keeping a tally of how you do in response to each question. All aspects of education have a strong core of accountability – the need to keep record, to be transparent – and so a grading of some kind throughout the interview is likely.

It means that if charisma has so far carried you through life, you must make sure you pay attention to the need to articulate specific experiences and a reflective outlook, both of which are likely to be pretty important to your interviewers.

The interview, in other words, isn't just about having the right personality, nor just 'knowing your stuff' or having a philosophy for your subject; it is about providing evidence of all of these.

So interviewers are likely to have criteria in which they are looking quite explicitly for some of the following:

- good interpersonal skills, with presence and confidence and an expressive, clear voice that is used effectively;
- the ability to be reflective and show good self-awareness;

Before training to teach

- a commitment to cope with the physical, emotional and intellectual demands of this Initial Teacher Training (ITT) programme;
- the resilience and tenacity to become a teacher.

Based on how well you match up to those expectations during the questioning and any other tasks that come your way, a decision will be made as to whether you will be offered a place on the training course.

TALKING POINTS

- How do you react to this set of criteria?
- Which parts are reassuring?
- How will you provide evidence of qualities such as being reflective and being resilient? What examples might you give from your life so far to show that you have the appropriate mindset and experience?

WHAT I DISLIKE ABOUT TEACHING

Work-life balance can be a real problem. There are periods when the pressure of work is pretty unbearable, and I can feel myself taking my stress out on people around me. Teaching seems to be like that – it has troughs and peaks, usually related to reports and exam periods, and you can feel that there's no escape from it all.

8 What to do if you are offered a training place

So, a letter arrives offering you a training place – whether based in a university or a school. What now?

If it's the place you want, accept it. Do so promptly and in the format that is requested – that is, in most cases, by signing an agreement, or in a letter of reply, or simply by confirming it online via UCAS.

Now your life is about to change, and you are likely, as you get nearer to the start date of your course, to feel some seismic shifts of emotions. You'll feel elated, terrified and all points in between.

There is stuff you could usefully be doing to start preparing yourself for the year ahead and in order to make your teacher training as personally rewarding and professionally productive as possible.

Here are two suggestions:

First, arrange some visits to schools. This may, in any case, be a prerequisite of the course you have just been accepted on to. Whether it is or not, the more you can immerse yourself in the culture of one or more schools, the better. If you can, get to watch a number of different teachers at work, including those outside your subject.

For example:

* To see how groups of students can be organised, given tasks and then be expected to work independently before

reporting back to the class, watch a great Drama teacher in action.

- To see the dynamic of group discussion being used to draw out students' ideas and then explore them in a calm, secure atmosphere, watch a great teacher of Personal, Social and Health and Economic Education (PSHE), Citizenship or RE.

- To see complex ideas explained in terms that make them simple, but not too simple, watch a great Science or History teacher.

- To see the power of end-of-lesson evaluations, reviewing what has been learned and what next steps are needed, watch a great teacher of Technology or PE.

- To see how students can benefit from individual feedback and be encouraged to explore new ideas, watch a great Art teacher at work.

- To see how a teacher can help students to think more precisely, building confidence through careful questioning, watch a great teacher of Mathematics at work.

- To see how a teacher makes explicit to students the implicit actions of literate adults – the techniques we deploy when reading and writing, for example – watch a great English teacher.

- To see how a teacher creates pace, variety, depth, reflection, purpose, calm and ongoing assessment, for a single class over a long period, go and watch a great primary teacher.

- To see the endless commitment and compassion of teachers in circumstances different from the ones you are soon to train for, try to watch a great special school teacher.

In other words, immersing yourself in the culture of classrooms is going to be hugely helpful, once you get started on your new career.

What to do if you are offered a training place

Remember that in schools it's not just the classroom that matters. All the other aspects of the role – being a tutor each morning, being on duty, eating lunch in the school dining hall – all of these can either carry a kind of mystique or provoke a sense of nervousness.

So get into a school and begin the process of absorbing the culture. This will help with the transition to your new working environment once your own teaching practice begins.

Next, start reading. The best teachers tend to combine deep knowledge of their subject with an ability to explain it in ways that students find compelling. In other words, they know a lot about what they teach and how they might teach it. You could usefully be doing some preparatory work on both aspects of becoming a teacher.

First, read more about your subject. Look at what the subject association (if there is one) has published. Look up the key writers on your subject. Learn about topics you have previously, at school or university, only skimmed. Start deepening your understanding, delving into some of the more obscure corners and more arcane topics.

Then, look at the ideas of the many educational writers who, in books and on blogs, have written about how to teach your subject. Blogging has been one of the most extraordinarily fertile areas in recent years, enabling ordinary teachers to exchange approaches and ideas. Start to get a feel for what they have to say.

You might also want to read books and articles on issues that are not specifically related to your subject but that will be relevant or simply interesting. These might be texts on literacy, or classroom management, or motivation, or on how the human brain works.

There is a list of recommended texts at the end of this book.

TALKING POINTS

- How keen are you to be accepted on to your chosen training course? How much does it matter to you?
- What are your contingency plans if you don't get accepted?
- If you do get on the course, how will your lifestyle be affected?

ADVICE FOR NEW TEACHERS

Make work-life balance a priority. You must take time off at the weekend (e.g. one day) and one evening a week. Go out, see friends, watch a film – remind yourself that there's a world out there.

Part II

Preparing for teaching practice

So, you've decided that teaching is the career for you. Now you need to become a really good teacher.

There are enough mediocre teachers in the profession – just as there are mediocre accountants, driving instructors and bankers in those professions.

In something as socially important as teaching, you don't just want to become a reasonable teacher, an 'okay' teacher, the kind of teacher who your students will put up with and then forget – you want to become a great teacher.

You'll need to work at it, adapt your approach, learn from mistakes, be thicker skinned, push through the frustrating parts of the job, and constantly learn.

The reward: being part of a great profession and knowing – just occasionally – that you've made a transformational difference to someone's life chances.

This short part is designed to help you acclimatise to the culture of your placement school as quickly as possible. It is written to help you to think through, in advance, some of the apparently trivial issues that often get overlooked – such as how to dress for teaching and where to eat at lunchtimes.

This is where your career as a future teacher really begins. Hold on tight . . .

9 How to prepare for visiting your placement school

Whichever route you are following into teaching, it's the experience you have in school that will have the greatest effect upon the kind of teacher you become. It is also likely to be the part of your training that, in the run-up to starting, fills you with most fear.

That's how we all felt.

Teaching practice is an essential part of becoming a teacher, because teaching is a job with so many variables – chiefly, the students. If you are training to work in an office, even in a high-powered role, there will be much to learn and many pressures to deal with, there is something about being in a school that makes training especially nerve-wracking.

That's because you are dealing with so many personalities – the students, but also the staff – all of whom will themselves have different concerns, hopes and expectations of what you might bring to the school.

School placement is the part of your training you are most likely to lose sleep about. So here are some hints on how to prepare.

First: know the school.

These days, it's easy to find out about the school in which you will be based for one of your teaching practice placements. You will, no doubt, be invited to have an initial exploratory visit. Don't rely on this to find out everything about the school. Look it up online in advance. Find out what it says about itself. Spend some time exploring its website, getting a sense of its values, skimming any policies it is likely to have online – in particular, policies for:

- uniform expectations
- behaviour
- rewards and sanctions.

You're not doing this to get any detailed grasp of what you will need to know once based in the school. It's more a case of orientating yourself psychologically – that is, getting a feel for the place and its values.

Such preparatory work will also help to establish a useful first impression when you visit the school and when someone mentions an aspect of the school's achievements or procedures. Being able to say – without seeming a smart alec – 'Ah, yes, I saw that on your website' will impress and show that you are someone who is likely to make a positive contribution to the school.

Second: ignore the naysayers.

Schools can exist in a climate of swirling rumours. If someone starts to tell you that the school you are placed in has a reputation for being rough, or for poor discipline, or for low morale, or for sliding inexorably down the league tables, ignore them.

If you swallowed everything you heard about UK schools, you'd think that most of them were under mob rule, peopled by hopeless teachers rejected from the cast of *Waterloo Road*.

The reality, as Ofsted has confirmed, is that the majority of schools in England are good or outstanding, and, whatever stories are passed around the community or by rival schools about poor behaviour, these are very rarely true.

Go into your new school preparing to see it through your eyes, not someone else's. But make sure you are going there having done some preliminary reading. And prepare to learn a lot.

TALKING POINTS

- What kind of school do you hope to go to for your first teaching placement? Why?
- What are the benefits in being assigned to a school that is quite different from the one you yourself attended?
- What does your initial research about the school (e.g. via its website) suggest about its values?

WHAT I LOVE ABOUT TEACHING

Working as part of a team. It can be full-on and pressurised, and sometimes tempers fray. But, at its best, you get to work with bright, sparky people in a job where you can see a real impact.

10 How to dress for teaching practice

Right – this is the point at which some readers or would-be readers browsing in a bookshop may start to part company with me. If you're going to be effective as a teacher, you have to dress like an effective teacher. This means on each day of your teaching practice; it means throughout the rest of your career.

Most schools will have a dress code, or at least a paragraph about their expectations of how staff should dress, and, more often than not, this will be published in the staff handbook. Chances are you will be given a copy on your first day of teaching practice.

But that may be too late, because you need to decide what to wear for that first day of teaching practice before you have visited the school.

My advice, which I've never wavered from, is, if in doubt, dress more formally than you might expect. First impressions matter in teaching more than in many careers, and if you turn up on day one looking too casual, you will, in the eyes of many students and staff, be branded a casual teacher.

At the schools I've worked in, I would expect that as a trainee teacher you would, if male, be wearing a formal shirt, a tie that is done up and probably a jacket, if not a suit. I'd expect female trainees to show a similar, equivalent level of formality – not dressing as if you were a pin-striped member of the school's leadership team, but certainly as someone who pays the school and me the respect of showing that you recognise our professional expectations of staff.

As our dress code for students forbids visible piercings, other than in the ears, we expect that of staff too.

Some people will give you different advice. Some schools will have alternative expectations. You will want to arrive at your own decision on how to dress for day one.

All I would say – as this book continually asserts – is that there is a symbolism to teaching, a sense that we mustn't just be good at teaching but also good at playing the part of the teacher: dressing in an appropriate, professional way is a key part of that symbolism.

TALKING POINTS

- Do you agree? Does the way you dress as a teacher really matter that much?
- Those teachers who influenced you in the past – how did they present themselves? Can you remember? Was it relevant?
- How do you intend to dress?

WHAT I DISLIKE ABOUT TEACHING

It can feel very political, with newspapers quoting ministers and other people who keep saying we're not doing well enough. Most of the time I can shrug it off, but just sometimes it can really get to you.

11

How to refer to yourself on teaching practice

This is an odd one, but a question that I remember fretting about when I trained in Leicester all those years ago. It was how to refer to myself.

What I worried about was how students would perceive me. If they thought I was the trainee teacher, would they simply see me as fair game for mischievous behaviour? Should I acknowledge I was just training, thereby inviting an element of being baited by the groups I taught, or should I try to swagger with the authority of being a real teacher?

That was an age before name badges. I certainly wouldn't want to have been given a badge declaring that I was a 'trainee'. It was a bit like at our school when we contemplated giving our trusty band of supply teachers badges saying, with admirable logic, 'supply teacher'.

We might as well have given them one saying 'victim': we would have undermined their classroom authority with what we wrote.

It's not that you don't want to acknowledge that you are a trainee teacher; rather, it's that you may not want to draw attention to it.

Of course, it may be that you have no such qualms about how you are perceived, and, in any case, it will depend on what your mentor or head of department does. It may be that she announces to the class you'll be taking over: 'This is Mr Nicholson. He's a trainee teacher who will be teaching you next term'.

In some schools that introduction would be lighting the blue touchpaper for jeers or groans; in others, almost certainly the majority, where training is long established, students may well be excited, or at least interested in the implications.

Or it may be that the students haven't been told anything other than that you – Mr Nicholson – will be teaching some of their lessons in the coming term.

My own suggestion is that when you meet a class for the first time, you have your name on display on the whiteboard and introduce yourself by saying something like:

> Good morning everyone. My name is Mr Barton. I'll be teaching you English for this term, sometimes team-teaching with Mr Palin, sometimes for parts of your lessons, and sometimes all of your lessons. Before being here I've worked in different places and am really looking forward to getting to know you and to helping you to do really well in English.

I think something like that gives an acknowledgement to students that it isn't business as usual and that you will be their new teacher; it avoids explicit reference to being a 'trainee' or 'student' teacher; and it provides a crisp and purposeful indication of how things will be on your watch.

TALKING POINTS

- Is this something you had thought about? Do you agree with the advice?
- If you have an unusual name, or one that will prove hard for students to say or spell, what might you do from the start of your time in school to help them to get to know it quickly?

12 How to have lunch

All right – I realise this is now starting to get silly. You didn't buy this book in order to read advice about eating lunch, right?

Here's why this topic is here:

School lunchtimes are an important indicator of what a school is really like – of how it operates, what its core values are, how the official expectations of behaviour and uniform hold up at a time when students have their most free time. In the best schools, it's probably the part of the school day when senior staff are most visible, making sure that the mood is calm and purposeful, ready for afternoon lessons.

For you, it's important that you make time to eat. The relentless pressure during teaching practice to be prepared for the next lesson, or to squeeze in a discussion with your mentor or head of department, can mean that you're lucky to grab a hasty sandwich.

This isn't helpful or healthy. Just as schools are defined by rhythms – of each day, each week, each term, each year – so you mustn't neglect your own body's need for refuelling.

Some days, inevitably, this will involve eating a sandwich in a departmental office or classroom. But try to make time also to get to the staffroom and, more importantly, to eat in the dining hall alongside students. This is important for various reasons.

First, we know that, amid the increasingly atomised lifestyles we lead, many people never sit and eat and talk together. Instead, they consume food while peering at a computer screen in various household locations, or they sit wordlessly perching food in front of them, while they watch television.

Often, it seems, the students who need most to learn to socialise effectively are the ones who get least practice. That's where school matters a lot, beyond the narrow confines of our classrooms and our subjects. In sitting and eating a meal, we are demonstrating something that many of us consider important and natural: we are modelling and communicating something that some students may too infrequently experience – the simple pleasure of a meal with friends.

If you can make time for it, you'll enjoy it, having a conversation with colleagues or students you may not know and will be contributing to something intangible but hugely important in the future lives of students.

TALKING POINTS

- So how does this advice feel? Wouldn't a sandwich in the staffroom suit better than eating in the school canteen?
- Or do you agree that having lunch alongside students may prove interesting and beneficial?
- What do you intend to do at lunchtimes?

13 How to use the staffroom

Staffrooms have, in many schools, changed or disappeared. Some larger schools and academies, in recognition of the increased pressures on teachers and perhaps an atomised way of working, have simply got rid of them. The concept of staff getting together over coffee during a morning break or lunchtime may, in these schools, feel laughably archaic.

In those schools where staffrooms remain, more often than not it may be a husk of the staff who are able to find the time or inclination to spend their break times there. There's too much to be done for to the next lesson, or students to see, or a trek to make across school.

In some ways, this is a pity, as one of the unrecognised benefits (though it can prove a drawback too) in the teaching profession is a now fading sense of collegiality – of being together with others who have a similar but different role and a shared sense of mission. A good staffroom gets you mixing with people who do different jobs from your own, teach a different subject and talk about different things.

A really good staffroom should, therefore, be a place of professional sustenance – allowing us to let off steam, to share ideas, to listen to the veterans of the classroom, to unwind and prepare for the next lesson.

Whether that is the case at your teaching practice school or not, my advice is to see the staffroom as an opportunity. If you're based in the school with other trainees, make an agreement that, on at least some occasions each week, you'll meet there. You need to do this because of the psychologically and emotionally draining nature of teaching. Camaraderie matters. Use the staffroom as a place where you at least occasionally meet at break and/or lunchtime, to build a deliberate reflective pause into your day and to unwind briefly.

Then go one stage further. If you are with other trainees, don't allow yourself to become part of an inevitable clique of newbies, who sit together, separate from other staff. Use the occasions to network a bit. Choose somewhere you haven't sat, next to someone you haven't sat next to and say, 'Hello, mind if I join you?' Then see what happens.

This sense of immersing yourself in a school's culture – through listening more than talking – is beneficial in further helping you to understand what being a teacher in this particular school is like, but also in giving you a broader perspective of the teaching profession.

The staffroom, therefore, isn't an ordeal to be endured, or a space to be avoided, or a haven where you just mix with like-minded rookies: it's an opportunity to accelerate your professional knowledge and understanding. Seize it.

TALKING POINTS

- Do you agree that showing you can integrate with other members of staff is important?
- How will you decide where to sit in the staffroom? Who, strategically, might you align yourself with in the early days – fellow trainees, a member of your new department, your mentor?

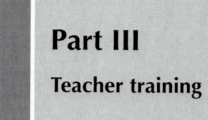

Part III

Teacher training

This is the core of the book, the section that drills into the essential skills you're going to need as a teacher. It is designed to complement what you learn as a trainee.

I have anchored the advice around the current Teachers' Standards – the nationally prescribed outline of what the Department for Education expects every teacher to know or do.

These are important and will be something that you return to throughout your career. For example, when you are part of the annual appraisal process in a school, it is against the Teachers' Standards that you will be expected to provide evidence of the impact you are making and the professional qualities you are displaying.

However, there's much more to being a great teacher than is contained in a centrally prescribed list of points. I will therefore cover much more than the Teachers' Standards require and, in particular, provide advice on issues that you are less likely to deal with in training and induction and yet are likely to keep you awake some nights with worry. These are issues such as behaviour management and dealing with difficult parents.

I have included a lot of guidance on behaviour management in particular, first, because it's something that worries people – the gnawing doubt about whether students will stop talking when you ask them to, whether they will do what you ask of them, whether you will have to deal with the riotous conduct that characterises the classrooms seen in most television depictions of school life.

The other reason there's a lot about behaviour is that good behaviour matters a lot: proper planned learning is unlikely to happen without it. A calm, orderly, supportive classroom ethos is a teaching essential, and it doesn't happen by accident. It is created.

This section will take you into the hidden heart of what great teachers do.

14 How to use the Teachers' Standards

The Teachers' Standards are designed to establish a national benchmark of what every student and parent ought to be able to expect from every teacher.

That sounds eminently sensible, you may feel.

Throughout your career as a teacher, you will be assessed against the Standards – or, at least, will be expected to provide evidence of how you meet or exceed the Standards.

It is, therefore, worth getting to know the Standards from the earliest stage of your career, which is why we are including most of them as the spine to this part of the book.

The Teachers' Standards fall into two parts: (1) teaching and (2) professional conduct. Here, we use them to explore some of the essential skills and approaches you will need as a new teacher and, a bit further down the line, will need to demonstrate during the process of performance review and appraisal.

TALKING POINTS

- What do you already know about the Teachers' Standards?
- What is the rationale behind them, do you think?

15 Using Teachers' Standard 1

How to set high expectations

Standard 1 starts, quite rightly, with our expectations as teachers. Here's what it outlines:

> Set high expectations which inspire, motivate and challenge pupils
>
> 1(a) establish a safe and stimulating environment for pupils, rooted in mutual respect
>
> 1(b) set goals that stretch and challenge pupils of all backgrounds, abilities and dispositions
>
> 1(c) demonstrate consistently the positive attitudes, values and behaviour which are expected of pupils.

Note the emphasis on safety from the very beginning of the Standards. This isn't a reminder just for those who will be teaching in science laboratories, technology workshops and the like. It's for all teachers, of all subjects, in all classrooms and in other spaces around school.

Safety will include setting expectations about how students behave, how they relate to each other and how they use social media. It's a reminder of the responsibility we have as adults to all the young people in our care – the importance of setting clear boundaries and giving students a clear, if implicit, sense that they can trust us and that they are safe.

46

Expectations are the key to this, and often, in the best lessons, it means expecting more than the students might expect of themselves. That will include being intolerant of poor behaviour and sloppiness and lateness – but doing so in a way, as the Standards state, that demonstrates mutual respect.

This is an area that, for new teachers, can prove the hardest balance to strike, and it's one we will return to in our later discussions of classroom practice. 'Mutual respect' certainly doesn't mean chumminess – that is, perceiving the role of the teacher as being a surrogate friend to the students. It doesn't mean turning a blind eye to inappropriate behaviour or cultivating informality.

Mutual respect will most easily be demonstrated in the way you address students, the way you greet them at your classroom door, the way you avoid the 'dark sarcasm of the classroom', even when having to express exasperation with a student who is misbehaving.

How might you demonstrate that you are meeting the Standard?

You could make sure that, in every lesson plan, you make a note of health and safety issues – showing how you explicitly pre-empt risks. In some subjects, this will be more pressing than others. In Science, for example, having a note relating to equipment and goggles will demonstrate your pre-emptive thinking.

In other subjects, it may be that there is no obvious safety risk that seems to need mentioning on the lesson plan. In this case, you might simply have a space in your planning template that says 'special safety concerns', in which you write 'none'.

In other words, health and safety – your responsibility for the care of students – are so important that even writing 'none' signals a level of deliberately reflective practice. It shows that safety has been considered, that it matters.

Notice, however, that the Standard is about another aspect of our core business as teachers: the expectations we set of our students, irrespective of their backgrounds and personalities. With this Standard, of course you will want to *do* that, but you will also need to provide ongoing evidence.

Sometimes, as soon as we talk about making sure that we have high expectations and challenge students, it's easy to assume that this means challenging our most academically able students and diluting those expectations for those who find the work hard.

The real test for us as teachers is to set work that is appropriately challenging for *all* our students.

It may be that your school has a house style on lesson objectives. Some expect a kind of three-level set of targets – what everyone in the group must achieve, what most might achieve and what some could achieve. These can feel a bit contrived.

Nevertheless, after establishing good behaviour, perhaps the most demanding part of a teacher's job is teaching in a way that challenges the range of students in a class. That doesn't mean – as we were once madly instructed – having an individual objective for each child. That would be impossible in most groups. It does mean demonstrating what you will do – and then have done – so that your ablest students feel challenged in a lesson and across a term, and the same for middle- and lower-ability students.

The longer you teach, the more intuitive this becomes.

You get to know more specifically what you might expect of students working at different levels of skill and knowledge. This, in turn, helps you to give them better quality feedback and, in due course, to be able to make suggestions to them as you move about the class about how they might improve their work.

But at this stage, you need to provide evidence that you are setting high expectations. Here's how to do this:

Make sure your lesson planning includes objectives or targets or a summary of knowledge and skills to be learned that are challenging. You might label them as such to make explicit that you are setting stretching tasks for students.

In your marking and feedback, mention from time to time where a student has responded at a high level to a challenging target.

Comment on how he or she has risen to the challenge and say 'well done'. Then, keep a copy of some examples of your marking in your portfolio (a single example won't be as persuasive as three to five examples from different groups).

Periodically – perhaps once each half-term – take a copy of a student response that exemplifies the high standards you have set. This won't only be in the content of the work that has been produced; it will show up in the presentation too. High expectations mean being persistent about how work should look – demanding high quality accuracy and clarity. This is particularly important from students whose backgrounds may not reinforce the high expectations you set.

Therefore, from time to time, take a copy as evidence of the high expectations you have of all your students. Keep it in a sub-section of your portfolio and label it something like 'Challenging Expectations'.

Finally, remember that any supportive comments students make about how you help them to improve their work – for example, in their written response to your marking, or in occasional emails or cards from them or their parents – are also important, objective sources of evidence for the high expectations you set.

It will seem, to some of us, a bit odd, even a bit cynical, to be saving these in a portfolio of evidence, but that is what we should do, because meeting the Teachers' Standards is something that needs to be built on a range of evidence rather than hearsay or reported good intentions.

TALKING POINTS

- What is your own experience of expectations – of parents and teachers who expected a lot from you, or expected too little?
- How would you characterise your own expectations of what all your students might achieve?

16 Using Teachers' Standard 2

How to help your students to achieve good progress

Standard 2 is fundamental to what great teachers do. Many of us have been taught by teachers who are entertaining, beguiling, compelling – but who ultimately don't help us to make the progress we ought to make.

'Progress' has become a slippery word in teaching, as we shall see, but here is how it is defined in the Teachers' Standards:

2(a) be accountable for pupils' attainment, progress and outcomes

2(b) be aware of pupils' capabilities and their prior knowledge, and plan teaching to build on these

2(c) guide pupils to reflect on the progress they have made and their emerging needs

2(d) demonstrate knowledge and understanding of how pupils learn and how this impacts on teaching

2(e) encourage pupils to take a responsible and conscientious attitude to their own work and study.

Promoting good progress is at the heart of a teacher's responsibilities. Of course we want to enthuse young people about our subject, or make them more rounded individuals, to develop their sense of self-esteem and build their character. Great teachers in great (and even in mediocre) schools do this.

However, we also need students to learn stuff – and to show that they have learned it.

These Standards, therefore, combine the need for you to know about how people learn and, specifically, how they learn in your subject, with the need to make sure you equip students with the skills and knowledge to demonstrate what they have learned.

It is easy to think about this purely in terms of preparing students for formal tests and examinations – these, after all, are the easiest way of being able to judge progress.

Whatever we might think of our cumbersome, clogged-up examination system, however frustrated we might feel about the annual pantomime of results days in which people lament falling standards or easier tests, however much all of this might feel alien to us and a sideshow – qualifications matter.

They matter because they open doors to the next phase of your life. Once you have got there, qualifications matter less. They fade into our personal backgrounds somewhat, referred to just occasionally in job applications and whenever our CVs have to be brandished.

So you don't want to be the kind of teacher who is seen merely as a brilliant entertainer, spinning plates in the classroom and gaining popular plaudits. You also have to make sure that your students achieve the results they are capable of – that they make progress that is, at the very least, what might be expected and, if you are genuinely an effective teacher, progress that is greater than we, or they, might have expected.

Great teachers help their students to achieve great results.

That means that part of your role is to make sure students are absolutely prepared for the tests and examinations they will face. And that, in turn, will mean building practice, more practice and then more practice into your teaching scheme.

You will want your students to go into any examinations feeling that they absolutely know the format of the examination, the nuances of the paper and the tips from an expert (you) on how they can best succeed.

Teacher training

So there is an important message here: don't be deceived into thinking that, for a teacher in a modern age, it is all about independent learning by students. We need to teach them, too – to instruct them, to show them how to do things and then to let them practise.

There will be times when we owe it to them to show that learning also contains strong elements of teacher instruction, sharply critical feedback, coaching, advice and – wait for it – tedium, because, if we genuinely want to prepare young people to be lifelong learners, then we must make sure we prepare them for the unspoken truth about learning. Sometimes, it's about routine and repetition and practice and boredom.

Having the resilience to know that and to keep trying is what will help them to become truly independent as learners – and to gain the qualifications they ought to get.

However, there is another dimension to the discussion of student progress and it goes to the heart of what a teacher's role is, because, in our exam-fixated education system, we can too easily equate progress only with external tests and assessment.

Much more important is that a teacher can see the progress a student is making within and between lessons. This is what a sports coach will routinely do – watch an athlete, give advice, urge practice, tweak technique, praise, chide, encourage, know when to push the player harder and when to ease off.

That metaphor of a coach can be a helpful one, because it's up to us, as teachers, to use our expertise to help the students in front of us learn what they need to learn and to identify whether they are doing so or not, and whether they are learning it fast enough or deeply enough, or whether there may be flaws in their skills and thinking.

This we might call 'assessment for learning', a phrase associated with a great academic who has written a lot about effective teachers and their use of assessment – Dylan Wiliam.

His ideas were misappropriated by some people to imply that it was a matter of representing students' progress in numeric levels.

You'd walk into a lesson and ask students what they were learning, and they would say things such as, 'Well, I was a level 4C and now I'm a borderline 5C'. Progress was reduced to something mechanistic, arid, soulless and often meaningless.

So we want all teachers to talk about real progress – the telltale signs by which students might show that they know more than they knew earlier and can do things they couldn't do previously.

If that sounds simple, it's not. But nor does it have to be complicated.

It's an issue we'll be addressing in this book and in the subject-specific companion titles.

For now, be aware of how central to your role student progress will prove, and heed a quick note of caution. Our obsession with measuring things in education has led many schools to believe that what Ofsted inspectors expect is to see twenty-minute chunks of progress.

That means that, in a brief period of being observed, there may be an expectation that, by the end of twenty minutes, your students will be able do something or explain something that they couldn't do twenty minutes earlier.

For some activities and topics, this is fine; for others, it will seem artificial.

So the advice here is: know what learning your subject entails. Think about the essential skills and knowledge people need to progress from novice to expert.

Visualise the building blocks and construct schemes of work, medium-term plans and lessons plans around them.

However, don't forget the bigger picture: we are engaged here in preparing young people for a world in which real learning won't be served up in self-contained chunks and pre-packaged, twenty-minute units.

As so often in teaching, therefore, it will be about striking a balance in the approaches you use.

Teacher training

How might you demonstrate that you are meeting the Standard?

You will want to use whatever information management system the school uses to demonstrate that the students you teach are making really good progress. This might be a page showing their prior attainment, their current attainment in your class, their targets and, in due course, their actual grade.

You might want to highlight those students who are doing better in your subject than in others, or those whose backgrounds mean that, at your school, they often underachieve.

All of this, in other words, will be about demonstrating numerically, or graphically, the progress your students make.

Of course, there may be some who will have disappointed you with their lack of progress. That is the nature of real teaching: we should not spoon-feed universal success. But you will want to show that, if there are underachievers in a class, these are counterbalanced by students who are making greater than expected progress.

Numbers, however, may not tell the whole story of the achievement of your students. Aim also to keep some examples of students' work. In particular, collect a few 'before and after' samples – examples of what some students were producing at the start of the year or term and what they are producing now.

The quality of presentation, the length of their work, the depth of their responses, the improvements in their use of vocabulary to explain concepts – all of these might serve as supporting evidence of what students taught by you can achieve.

You will also want to provide evidence that you know how people learn in your subject and to demonstrate that students taught by you are showing increasing levels of independence in their progress.

Look out for opportunities to hold on to a scheme of work or lesson plan where you have a specific concept that you are teaching – something that is essential for all students to learn (such as the concept of proportionality in maths). In your planning, show ways that you will make the concept more accessible – through an explanation, diagram or metaphor (linking the concept to some other idea to help illuminate it).

Keep an example of some planning that has an explicit approach to developing students' independent learning. If independence is a skill you wish to develop explicitly, tell the students this at the start of the project. Then, once the work is completed, ask students to do some self-evaluation. Get them to respond to the content – the 'what' of the work – but ask them also to write down something about 'how' they approached the task, what they learned and how they managed their time and study more independently.

Some of these comments should provide you with an example that you can photocopy and add to your portfolio. The aim: to show that you had planned for student independence and that, at the end of the sequence, there is evidence of it (in the work) and of an increasingly independent approach (in the commentary).

There will be other evidence you may want to keep to show students' progress and mastery of skills. Your markbook, for example, will be an important way of highlighting the progress of students generally and specific groups of students.

Just don't underestimate the significance of being able to present a photocopy of a student's classwork, homework or planner. Build into your teaching times when they – not you – are annotating work or providing a commentary on what decisions they have made and their reflections on both *what* and *how* they have learned.

Remember that this shouldn't be an onerous, last-minute scramble. Aim, once a half-term or so, to collect two or three pieces of evidence that demonstrate the progress both you and your students have made. Photocopy it; file it; make it an ongoing dimension of the way you work.

That is, build it into your routines.

TALKING POINTS

- Earlier I described progress as a slippery term: what do you understand by this?
- So, what was your own experience of 'progress' at school? How did you know when you were doing something better? What kind of feedback helped you most?
- What is your experience of 'progress' in your training so far?

ADVICE FOR NEW TEACHERS

Use other people's resources. There are so many out there – you don't have to constantly reinvent the wheel. And try to be systematic in saving the materials you produce. It makes it so much easier if you can quickly find them again the following year.

17 Using Teachers' Standard 3

How to demonstrate good knowledge of your subject

Occasionally, you may find yourself embroiled in a rather fatuous argument about how important knowledge is. You will hear people arguing that we live in an age in which knowledge changes so rapidly that trying to 'know stuff' is impossible.

Instead, they argue, our role as teachers is to help students know how to find knowledge.

There is something beguiling about this line of argument: it is easy to swallow its logic.

In reality, although knowledge might be constantly being reformulated on the outer edges – the places where researchers are testing hypotheses and undertaking complex experiments – it won't affect what most of us are doing in our classrooms.

Boyle's Law, after all, is Boyle's Law, and *The Merchant of Venice* is *The Merchant of Venice*, even though new insights, approaches and interpretations might nudge on some of our understanding.

In this, knowing things in the first place provides the building block for building further knowledge. Thus, the student who knows things, who has some general knowledge, is going to be at a huge advantage. The idea that all lessons can be about how to use Google or evaluating the reliability of different Wikipedia pages will do students few favours. We need also to teach them stuff.

This is where teacher knowledge comes in.

Teacher training

Here is what the Teachers' Standards require:
Teachers should:

3(a) have a secure knowledge of the relevant subject(s) and curriculum areas, foster and maintain pupils' interest in the subject, and address misunderstandings

3(b) demonstrate a critical understanding of developments in the subject and curriculum areas, and promote the value of scholarship

3(c) demonstrate an understanding of and take responsibility for promoting high standards of literacy, articulacy and the correct use of standard English, whatever the teacher's specialist subject

3(d) if teaching early reading, demonstrate a clear understanding of systematic synthetic phonics

3(e) if teaching early mathematics, demonstrate a clear understanding of appropriate teaching strategies.

A few years back, Ian Gilbert wrote a book called *Why do I Need a Teacher When I've Got Google?* It's a great title that raises a question that we all ought to be asking in a period when information is so easy for all of us to find, irrespective of our teachers.

My guess is that social media, a stronger emphasis on individuality and a culture that gives more attention to young people – all of these have contributed to students being less tolerant of mediocre teaching.

When I was at school, quality control was an unheard-of term, as well as a rare concept in school. Who you got as a teacher was part of the lottery of the education system.

Now, in schools, we try to do more to manage the performance of teachers, to improve the weaker ones and to harness the talents of the best. More of that later.

My point is this: there is no need for students to tolerate poor teaching, if they can access the knowledge they need by circumventing us.

However, I also suspect that we all still love the human dimension of being taught by a great teacher. There's a sense of excitement that few websites will emulate. And, in general, great teachers will know their subject very well.

Teacher knowledge is undoubtedly a key ingredient in being a really successful teacher, but note that it isn't, on its own, enough.

I'll guess that we have all been taught by teachers who knew a lot about mathematics or science or English. And we often hated their lessons.

That's because teacher knowledge only takes us so far.

As our experience of being taught by truly great teachers demonstrates, it is about a passion for, as well as knowledge of, the subject. Great teachers know a lot, but they are also endlessly restless, wanting to keep knowing more. They read about it. They talk about it. They enjoy being asked questions they hadn't thought about – they like having their own knowledge challenged and pushed.

One of the least publicised pleasures of teaching is how this deepens and enriches our love of our subject. You find yourself getting more interested in more obscure aspects of the subject, because teaching it requires you to find 'ways in' for students not yet smitten by the bug. Pedagogy – the how of teaching – deepens our reflection, gets us really thinking about the best way to help students to absorb, practise and memorise the skills and knowledge they need.

How might you demonstrate that you are meeting the Standard?

As we have been saying, good subject knowledge is important for being a really good teacher. It just isn't enough, on its own, to guarantee that you are a really good teacher. It's what you do with that knowledge, how you impart it and how you use a range of approaches to render complicated stuff simpler and more accessible.

This Standard requires evidence of subject knowledge. You may have qualifications, or a certificate or two about a key aspect of the

Teacher training

subject, or you may have attended a training course. All of these will count as evidence of your subject knowledge.

I would also expect that you will be passionate about your subject and that you should keep up to date with any developments within it. One way is by joining a subject association. Organisations such as the National Association for Teachers of English and the Association of Science Educators will provide you with website updates and occasional printed material, which could be invaluable for seeing how your subject is developing and what the main themes and concerns are.

You may have attended conferences or 'teach meets', in which case bring back a certificate of attendance and, if travelling by train, take ten minutes to summarise what you gained from the course. As ever, put this straight into your portfolio of evidence.

Notice also, quite rightly, the emphasis on every teacher having knowledge beyond his or her own subject. This is where whole-school literacy is especially important, and you could provide evidence of:

- the formative nature of your marking (e.g. you make a comment suggesting how the students might improve; in reply, the students make a comment showing their under-standing of your advice and what they intend to do as a result);

- how your written feedback or any handouts you have produced help students to build their vocabulary, structure sentences and spell more accurately;

- schemes of work or lesson plans that explicitly reference literacy – for example, the words and phrases you will deliberately be teaching students;

- examples of any training attended on whole-school literacy or numeracy;

- samples of students' work from the start and later stages of the year that demonstrate the impact of your teaching, both in your subject and in their wider knowledge, such as speaking, reading and writing better.

TALKING POINTS

- Who are the teachers who had the biggest impact on you? Were they the most knowledgeable?
- Where do you stand on the 'skills versus knowledge' debate, or do you think it is a phoney one? Why?

WHAT I LOVE ABOUT TEACHING

Working with young people. I find I learn so much from them. It's made me appreciate more about how we learn and what the barriers are. I've definitely become more self-aware about my own learning.

18

Using Teachers' Standard 4

How to plan and teach well-structured lessons

The best lessons will usually – though actually not always – be well planned.

That doesn't, however, mean that they will follow some robotic formula that begins with a learning objective and ends with a plenary activity. As you develop your confidence and expertise as a teacher, you'll move away from very predictable lesson plans to those that may be more organic, which will allow you to follow the response of the students more sensitively.

This isn't the same as saying that as you become more authoritative in the classroom, you'll start to abandon lesson plans.

Instead, it's a recognition that, as we become increasingly proficient at a skill, and the more knowledgeable we become about a topic, the less we have to labour over mapping out the mechanics of delivery.

When you cook a new recipe, you will, in the early attempts, be slavishly faithful to the writer's instructions. As you internalise the list of ingredients, routines, timings and advice, you will move away from the writer's inky words and rely more on your own internalised approach.

This is how lesson planning is likely to develop.

In your earliest days as a fledgling teacher, your lesson plans will exemplify the step-by-step ingredients in your thinking. You are likely to over-plan. I hope that's the case, because the importance of planning isn't just for the lesson plan you have in front of you when you teach a lesson.

It also represents a thought process, a way of thinking.

Planning those early lessons, laboriously and neurotically, into the early hours of too many mornings is training us to be a better planner of lessons – it is building our confidence and professional assurance. It is helping us to internalise, for the career that lies ahead of us, one of the most fundamental skills you will need as a teacher.

So notice what I am saying and what I am not: planning is important, but, as you get better at it, so your planning will become less formulaic, less detailed, and will be transformed into a template rather than a checklist.

Most important is to know who your plan is for: is it designed to illuminate the understanding of an observer – someone who is definitely or possibly coming in to observe you? If the audience is a public one like that, then your lesson plan will need to communicate certain essential information:

- who the class is, the range of abilities and target groups it contains (e.g. children with special needs, children deemed by the school to be on free school meals, and suchlike);

- what the students have previously done – a sentence giving the context of how this lesson builds on what they did previously;

- a learning objective of some sort – in other words, what students are expected to have learned by the end of the lesson; the plan will contain a sequence of activities and tasks, but these should be built around learning – a precise statement of the skills and knowledge that all students, perhaps to differing degrees, should have mastered by the end of the lesson;

- a sequence of activities briefly listed;

- for me, always, a list of the key vocabulary students should understand and use in order to demonstrate their growing ability to speak, read and write like a historian, musician, mathematician and so on.

A lesson plan for an audience other than you is likely to require other elements – equipment needed, timings and suchlike. However, if it is genuinely a lesson plan, a template for the lesson that you will teach, then design it with that practical notion in mind. Use it as a working document, with reminders to yourself of things you shouldn't forget.

The other point about lesson plans is that, in your early days, they are likely to be somewhat different from those in the later stages of your career – by which I mean you in a year or two's time. When we are learning to teach, we are likely to need to plan our approach much more explicitly. We are still learning our craft. In the process, through repetition and modifying approaches based on errors, you will be building various routines that you may well continue to use for the rest of your teaching life.

In the early stage of your career, as you forge these habits, you will be writing them down. Soon enough you won't need to. Future lesson plans, therefore, may become more minimalist but possibly more ambitious: as you develop your ability to organise students in different groups, to explain concepts better, to be secure in your ability to innovate, so your lesson plans will take on a new shape.

For now, keep them clear, logical, easy to follow, with a straightforward arc of time management that will take the class reassuringly from the start of the lesson to a satisfying conclusion in which they know things and can do things that, an hour or so earlier, they didn't or couldn't.

Here is what the Teachers' Standards require:

Teachers should:

4(a) impart knowledge and develop understanding through effective use of lesson time

4(b) promote a love of learning and children's intellectual curiosity

4(c) set homework and plan other out-of-class activities to consolidate and extend the knowledge and understanding pupils have acquired

4(d) reflect systematically on the effectiveness of lessons and approaches to teaching

4(e) contribute to the design and provision of an engaging curriculum within the relevant subject area(s).

How might you demonstrate that you are meeting the Standard?

You should add to your portfolio a small number of examples of your planning. Include in this something that shows how you plan over the long- or medium-term – in other words, how you can take the core skills and knowledge of your subject and organise the activities that will help students to build their mastery over a longer sequence of lessons.

Include something that demonstrates how you can take an especially important topic from your subject and help students to master it as the result of a short-term plan – within one lesson.

If you can, noting what this Standard is looking for, include an example where you have planned a lesson or activity that contributes to a whole-school theme or priority. It might be that you have been involved in a cross-curricular day or a student conference. Or it might be that you have taught a topic that has at its core an important aspect of literacy, numeracy, citizenship or PSHE.

The point is: show that you can plan lessons and have some well-chosen, representative samples that go beyond the confines of one lesson and, ideally, beyond the confines of your subject.

One other thing: experience tells me that there isn't always an automatic correspondence between brilliant lesson planning and brilliant teaching. It is rare to see a really good lesson where you can't also sense a very strong, well-thought-out, underpinning rationale. It is less rare to see a highly detailed lesson plan and yet to be sitting in the actual lesson that it is supposed to represent and feel that it is tedious or unchallenging or on the brink of mayhem.

So keep your eye on impact: what does your lesson planning lead to? How does it help students to become more engaged with the topic and to learn more and to learn faster? How might you show that?

As part of your portfolio, include some student feedback. I recommend that, at the end of every topic, you do some form of student evaluation. This use of 'punter feedback' will help you to know (a) what students enjoyed and didn't enjoy (which may not be as important as you think), but also (b) what they thought went too quickly or too slowly.

Student feedback is important because it can help us to get an insight from the viewpoint of the novice (the student) rather than the expert (us). It can help to recalibrate our planning – to see that there might be a skill or activity that needs more or less time allocated to it.

So, when putting together a student evaluation – which may simply be three or so questions at the end of a half-term or a taught unit – ask a question related to planning. It might be something direct like this:

> How well planned did the lessons on this unit feel to you?
>
> 1 (not very) ––– 5 (very)
>
> Explain why:

Alternatively, you might ask them for a more detailed response:

> The planning for this topic included X, Y and Z. Did we spend the right amount of time on each of these elements? Should we have done more on some things and less on others? What advice would you give me on the planning and timing for next time I teach the topic?

Teachers sometimes worry about using this kind of feedback. Personally, I don't. After all, the best teachers worry obsessively about their teaching. Student evaluations can help us to make the details of our teaching better and better; they can also serve as helpful evidence of the impact of our planning, which is why I recommend you choose one or two positive examples to add to your portfolio of evidence for how you are meeting the Teachers' Standards.

One last suggestion: as a trainee or rookie teacher, you're going to be observed a lot. Nudge your mentor to comment on your planning – in particular, how the plan you have on paper is then translated by you into an effective, well taught lesson. If this is what she sees, ask her to write it down on the observation form (if she hasn't).

Hang on to that sheet as another piece of evidence of the impact of your planning. Cling on to it also as a reminder, on one of those dark evenings when one of your lessons has imploded around you, that you do know how to plan, that you are effective, but that, in the real world sometimes, as the poet Robbie Burns taught us, 'the best laid schemes o' mice an' men' can fall apart.

That's teaching – in all its naked charm and occasional horror.

TALKING POINTS

- What do you understand about the distinction between a good lesson plan and a lesson that has been well planned?
- Which aspects of lesson planning do you currently find most challenging?
- Have you had the opportunity to work with an established teacher on the way she plans? If not, who would you choose?

19

Using Teachers' Standard 5

How to adapt your teaching to respond to the strengths and needs of all students

As a rule, less effective teachers will write pretty good lesson plans. Then they will slavishly teach them. And, in that way, the quality of the lesson may end up as mediocre.

As we have already said, an effective lesson plan doesn't automatically translate into effective teaching. The problem lies, of course, in the implication of the word 'slavishly' above.

A lesson plan comes to life in the classroom: it translates into a sequence of questions and activities that lead to students knowing some stuff that they didn't know before and doing some things that they couldn't do earlier.

Put simply, this is how a lesson plan translates into effective teaching, which leads to successful learning.

The plan is your template, but it's what you do in the classroom that counts. That's where shaping the lesson around the strengths and needs of all students is so important.

This can be a daunting prospect. Graham Nuthall exposes this in his brilliant book of research, *The Hidden Lives of Learners* (2007):

> In most of the classrooms we have studied, each student already knows about 40 to 50 per cent of what the teacher is teaching ... We have found that individual students can learn quite different things from the same classroom activities because

they begin the activity with distinctly different background knowledge and experience the activity differently.

We will never know each student's prior knowledge in a way that is meaningful enough for us to tailor the content of the lesson precisely to their needs. However, the important starting point is the recognition that what we have in front of us is not just a class, a group, but rather a collection of individuals, some of whom may be capable of very high levels of skill and understanding, and others who may need support.

From the outset, you'll want to be thinking in terms of what to do to build in a level of appropriate challenge that will stretch all the students before you. It means that your input as a teacher might quite legitimately be posing a big question, explaining something and pointing out clearly what you expect all students to be able to demonstrate by the end of the lesson and unit.

However, you will then tailor your teaching to specific groups of individuals through, for example, keeping one group that needs more guided teaching with you in order to explain further and take and ask questions. You might set some students some additional reading or research, or expect a higher level of precision in what they produce. This, in other words, is where a skilful teacher will tailor their input to the students in front of them.

Here's how the approach is outlined in the Teachers' Standards: Teachers should:

5(a) know when and how to differentiate appropriately, using approaches which enable pupils to be taught effectively

5(b) have a secure understanding of how a range of factors can inhibit pupils' ability to learn, and how best to overcome these

5(c) demonstrate an awareness of the physical, social and intellectual development of children, and know how to adapt teaching to support pupils' education at different stages of development

5(d) have a clear understanding of the needs of all pupils, including those with SEN; those of high ability; those with EAL; those with disabilities; and be able to use and evaluate distinctive teaching approaches to engage and support them.

This is one of the most challenging aspects of teaching. It may be helpful to group approaches around four themes:

(a) Differentiation by resource:

Here, you use different materials according to the needs of different students. Some examples: resources are related to different readability levels – with more challenging texts for some students. Or you provide an additional handout, a glossary of key words, a set of instructions, or a model or demonstration to help those students needing support.

For the ablest students, your additional resources might model what a top-level response looks like and get them to review and critique it.

(b) Differentiation by task:

Here, you expect different groups of students to work on different tasks. You might give the choice of tasks to students or you might direct them to the task most suited to their needs. What you want to beware of is the ablest students completing a challenging piece of writing while the less able are doing a word search. Left to our own choices, it might be that unconfident learners will default to the task they perceive to be 'easier' or that involves less reading or writing.

Here, then, is where you will want to plan tasks that contain challenge and that have clearly defined outcomes, and you will want to guide students to the one that will stretch the aspect of learning they most need to develop.

(c) Differentiation by support:

This is where you, or a student mentor, or a teaching assistant, can use your teaching skills, your questioning and explanation to work with individuals and small groups.

It's also where you might look at how you group students, sometimes putting together those who are struggling with a concept so that you can give them additional teaching, and sometimes deploying those in the group who are the 'experts', so that they model the skills necessary.

Again, don't try to make this up on the spot: plan in advance the groupings and interventions that are most likely to help a student build necessary skills and knowledge.

(d) Differentiation by response:

Here is where feedback is so important, helping a student to see how well she is doing and what areas she needs to work on next.

This is where you are spelling out in advance what you expect in terms of an outcome from different groups. We need to be a bit careful with this, because it can imply that, from the outset, we are writing off some students as never to be able to make the top grades or to demonstrate outstanding achievement.

It might, therefore, be better to articulate what top-level performance looks like and what you need to do to get there, and then to talk in terms of the areas that people learning the skill find difficult. This is how sports coaching works – looking at the barriers to progress, working on them through practice and giving frequent feedback.

So it may be that students use individual action plans or learning logs to reflect upon and explain what they are finding easy and difficult, so that you can then suggest what they need to do next to improve.

Teacher training

All of this is a reminder that some of your most powerful teaching may well not be done in front of the whole class. Instead, it will be where you work with individuals or small groups, looking at the work they are completing, asking them questions to clarify their understanding and explaining areas that they aren't yet grasping.

This is teaching that is directed to the needs of the group. It isn't to say that whole-class teaching isn't a good idea. Of course it is. But, however skilful your explanation and questioning, it will need the guided teaching element – by you or a teaching assistant – to really make the impact of your teaching more secure for the full range of students in the group.

As you become more experienced as a teacher, you will get better at this. You will learn which concepts and skills hold the greatest difficulties for students. You'll learn about techniques to simplify some concepts, without oversimplifying them, or develop ways to help students memorise certain bits of knowledge.

You'll learn through experience how best to deploy a teaching assistant: whether she works one-to-one with a specified student, either in the room or elsewhere; whether she works with a small group; whether she re-teaches a concept you have introduced or oversees students having their first go at responding to the challenge at the heart of the lesson.

Your approach might entail having an additional activity that some students do – something that bridges the easier and more challenging parts of the lesson content.

It might be that you organise the groups or pairs in the lesson to have students who have 'got it' working with those who have 'not yet got it'. It might be that, having explained clearly the activity that the group is working on for the next twenty minutes or so, you then bring together the four or five students who you know will struggle and you give them extra teaching.

I refer to this as 'guided teaching' and find it the most helpful element in my own teaching. It builds in an extra stage for a small group of students when I – not a teaching assistant or other adult – can work at the front of the classroom with those students who are likely otherwise to sit with that 'I can't do this' look in their eyes or drift into distraction. Instead, they get extra teaching and an opportunity to ask questions that they might have been self-conscious about asking in front of the whole group.

How might you demonstrate that you are meeting the Standard?

Here's one where you might want to keep some lesson plans that you have subsequently annotated, to demonstrate how you adapted your teaching to meet the needs of the group.

That happened to me yesterday: what I had planned with a Year 11 English class was to work on some past examination questions. However, when we discussed how they had got on with their homework, it was clear that they were struggling with finding appropriate quotations.

We therefore changed tack, put the students into groups of three, with each group taking responsibility for making notes and finding quotations about each character, and then collated their findings into a booklet that they could download and revise from.

The lesson was thus diverted from what I had planned, and it was better as a consequence, more suited to what students needed at that point in their development.

I then annotated the lesson plan kept it as a record.

I would also suggest that you use your termly or half-termly student evaluation sheets to ask the question, 'Do you feel my lessons adapt to your needs?' or similar. If students are saying that they don't, then it will help you to become more confident about responding to needs; if they say yes, then the evidence will be useful for meeting the Teachers' Standard.

Teacher training

TALKING POINTS

- What do you already do in your planning to adapt your teaching to the full range of student abilities in your group? How effective are you?
- How do you feel about the suggestion of using questionnaires as a source of developmental feedback on the impact of your teaching?

WHAT I DISLIKE ABOUT TEACHING

There's so much paperwork. I really hate it. It can feel like it's sapping all my creativity. It may be that I'm not much good at managing admin, but frankly it just feels that there's too much of it, and it distracts me from the stuff that matters.

20 Using Teachers' Standard 6

How to assess students accurately

Assessment is a key part of what every teacher does. It is easy, in these days of constant tracking and monitoring of students' performance, to think of it in narrowly mechanistic terms, to think of figures on a spreadsheet. It is easy, too, to think that it is all about the 'high stakes' stuff – the exam results and school performance tables.

However, genuine assessment is richer and more nuanced than that and, at its best, will inform your teaching, as well as helping students to know how they are progressing.

At its best, assessment will also blend with your teaching. You will explain things, set tasks and then use questioning and ongoing assessment tasks to help your students to see how they are doing. This is the assessment that is most going to help them to make progress.

So, from the outset, we make a distinction between two broad forms of assessment:

Formative assessment

This is ongoing assessment designed to monitor student learning and to provide feedback that will help students to improve their learning. Although it may include some numeric mark or level, it ought to go beyond this. Telling a student that he is a C- and needs to work towards C+ won't help him much, unless there is some outline of what he needs to do to make progress. The best formative assessment is, therefore, often written or spoken advice on what to do more of ('use more interesting, varied connectives') or do less of ('use the words "and" and "but" less').

This is important to the student, but will also inform our teaching: it will help us to know whether, for some students in the group, we need to speed up, slow down, emphasise certain skills and knowledge more or re-teach some concepts.

Good quality assessment will feed into our planning and teaching, and, of course, some of the ongoing, formative assessment will be done by the students – assessing each other's work against criteria you give them or assessing their own work to articulate how they are doing and where they are having difficulties.

This is true assessment for learning.

Summative assessment

Summative assessment evaluates student learning at the end of a topic or unit by comparing it against some standard or benchmark. It's going to show the student and teacher how successfully something has been learned. It will receive a grade or level.

Here is what the Standards require:

Teachers should:

6(a) know and understand how to assess the relevant subject and curriculum areas, including statutory assessment requirements

6(b) make use of formative and summative assessment to secure pupils' progress

6(c) use relevant data to monitor progress, set targets, and plan subsequent lessons

6(d) give pupils regular feedback, both orally and through accurate marking, and encourage pupils to respond to the feedback.

Implications for you

These Standards relate to an earlier set – Standard 3: demonstrating good subject knowledge. That is because, as a teacher of your subject, you will need some conception of what doing better in it looks like. What are the skills and knowledge that most tangibly signify that we are getting better at it? In English, for example, one key indicator of growing mastery of writing is the ability to write in more complex sentences, linking ideas with connectives other than 'and' and 'but'.

Here is a simple demonstration. These two sentences demonstrate what progress looks like in writing:

- Sentence (a): 'I enjoy playing tennis, but I generally prefer squash.'

- Sentence (b): 'Although I enjoy playing tennis, I generally prefer squash.'

As a teacher of English, I therefore know that teaching more complex sentence structure and equipping students with a richer range of connectives ('although', 'because', 'after', 'however', 'while' and so on) will improve their writing. This therefore informs my teaching.

However, I also know that, when assessing students' progress – whether in their spoken English or writing – I will be looking for evidence of these syntactic features. It's what will help me to see whether a student is beginning to demonstrate writing that is more complex.

So, what might this mean in our classrooms?

Here's an underlying sequence for assessment that is built around learning:

Big picture

At the start of a unit of work or lesson, you will want to articulate the outcome of the learning – what students will know or be able to do at the end of the process. You need to be clear about how they will demonstrate this learning. You will want to show them the criteria by which they will be assessed. This is mapping out the big picture, the trajectory that the learning will take.

Exemplar material

As part of the process, you will want to enable students to see an exemplar of what they are aiming towards. Increasingly, it seems to me that every classroom should have on display a sample essay or assignment that demonstrates top quality work, annotated to show why it is so good.

However, bad models can also be unexpectedly helpful – looking at (anonymous) samples of work that aren't at the highest level and getting students to explore and interrogate these.

Knowing what they are aiming for and seeing samples of work that don't match those standards can be a really helpful way of building students' more precise understanding of what they are aiming for.

Practice

This will be the core of the lesson or unit of work, with students using the big picture, the assessment criteria and the exemplars and then starting to practise the skill for themselves.

This is where learning should be happening, and it may well be messy, with students making mistakes, getting frustrated, making small steps and gradually gaining confidence as they realise that they can do what has been set.

It should be accompanied by opportunities for precise, specific feedback, from you, or other adults, or other students.

Feedback

Whether it's using criteria or level descriptors, or looking at what a student is producing and asking questions and giving feedback, this is where the process of fine-tuning a student's response can happen.

Increasingly, as an English teacher, I do a lot of marking with students beside me. I can explain where I don't understand a point, where there's a clumsiness or inaccuracy in expression, where certain parts of the writing work really well.

The student, in this way, gets to see and hear what it is that we are looking for, as the experts in our subject, and I can give more directed guidance on what she needs to practise next.

Summative assessment

The process will end in a product – an artefact, a design, a piece of writing, a presentation, a performance – which is the culmination of this whole process. This is where you will be assessing it formally, so that the student knows how good it is.

However, that really shouldn't be the end of the process. If you stick a grade on the work, the risk is that students lock on to that and see it as a final, unmovable judgement. It may well be. But you need to provide some summative comment that helps them to see how you reached your decision and suggests what the student could do next time to do better. A comment or question that then expects the student to respond to your evaluation will help to make it a process of ongoing reflection.

So, after your grade or mark and comment, expect the student to respond. What was he pleased with? What could he have done better? What are the main skills or areas of knowledge he has learned?

How might you demonstrate that you are meeting the Standard?

You will want to show that your marking is effective in helping students to make progress. When you mark books, you will probably want students to respond. You might ask them a question

Teacher training

– 'What specifically could you have done to make your ideas clearer here?' – and expect them to write a response at the start of the next lesson.

In this way, marking becomes more of a dialogue between you and the student. Keep some copies of marking that you think exemplifies this process – where a student has responded to what you have asked or suggested and where, in the next piece of work, you can see that she has made progress as a result.

Be ready to demonstrate that students from different backgrounds and of different abilities do well as a result of your teaching and feedback. Have a spreadsheet of results to show it – especially how you cater for gifted and talented students and those with special needs. Keep evidence of how Pupil Premium students progress in your classroom.

Finally, use regular student surveys in which you ask each class to give you a comment or a grade on aspects of your teaching, including assessment. Be bold about this: if you wish to keep improving as a teacher, you'll want to have regular, honest feedback from your students.

You might, therefore, use a questionnaire that includes questions such as these:

- Do you find my marking helpful? (not very) 1 2 3 4 5 (very)
- How could I improve the feedback I give you?

Completed once a term, as part of your ongoing self-evaluation, this will help you to improve in this key area of your teaching and will provide you with useful evidence for appraisal of the impact your assessment has for students.

TALKING POINTS

- Think back to how assessment worked for you at school: can you remember teachers who gave ongoing formative feedback that shaped your progress, or is it just the summative assessment that sticks?
- Looking through the teacher comments scattered through this text, it's the pressure of marking books that is their biggest complaint. What alternatives to marking can you immediately think of?

ADVICE FOR NEW TEACHERS

Do as much marking as possible alongside pupils, to give maximum impact for them and to address their misconceptions. I find I learn a lot from marking in this way and it also helps the students to explain where they got stuck.

21 Using Teachers' Standard 7

How to establish (and maintain) effective classroom discipline

This is the topic that worries would-be teachers more than any other. In fact, it worries all of us – the new kids on the block and the most seasoned of veterans. We'll mention it here, and then we'll come back to the topic later in this part of the book.

Teaching is unlike many other jobs, in that it isn't just something you do sitting at a desk or interacting with a team of colleagues. There is also this whole expectation that a group of up to thirty young people will be quiet and attentive in your presence. Whatever the stage we are at in our careers, we worry that sometimes they won't.

Managing good behaviour understandably forms one of the Teachers' Standards:

Teachers:

7(a) have clear rules and routines for behaviour in classrooms, and take responsibility for promoting good and courteous behaviour both in classrooms and around the school, in accordance with the school's behaviour policy;

7(b) have high expectations of behaviour, and establish a framework for discipline with a range of strategies, using praise, sanctions and rewards consistently and fairly;

7(c) manage classes effectively, using approaches which are appropriate to pupils' needs in order to involve and motivate them;

7(d) maintain good relationships with pupils, exercise appropriate authority, and act decisively when necessary.

So, how do we develop approaches and routines that are likely
to lead to positive behaviour from students?

It can sometimes be counter-productive to watch really effective
teachers at work. We can watch them with even the most
challenging of groups and be drawn into the sense of mystery they
exude.

When I was on teaching practice, many years ago, at a comprehensive school in Leicester, I watched my mentor, Bryan Palin,
with a Year 8 group that had a pretty dodgy reputation.

At the end of the lesson, he needed them to be quiet, so that
he could explain their homework. He stood and looked at them. He
waited briefly. They fell silent. It was like watching a master
conjuror at work, or a lion tamer.

He was doing something that looked so effortless and yet so
unattainable that I almost felt like giving up on my chosen
profession there and then.

So beware of watching charismatic teachers in full flow. Often,
they will have been long established in the school, their reputations
known by a previous generation of students and, in turn, by those
students' parents.

Or it may be that they have roles in school that automatically
bestow a kind of unspoken authority on them – as heads of year,
for example, or similar roles that, in the eyes of the students, mean
that these people wield intangible power.

No – far better to watch a teacher who uses techniques rather
than the mysteries of personality to achieve high quality classroom
discipline.

Fundamental to this will be 'withitness' – that sense of being
attuned to the mood of the class, sensing when the pace is dropping,
pre-empting a student who is drifting off task and about to do
something foolish.

Withitness is, perhaps, our most important asset as teachers.

Teacher training

We learn it by spending time in lessons and getting a feel for how children behave. We learn it by knowing how to divert a student or a group from one task to another, how to increase pace and rejuvenate the energy of a classroom.

The insights into this comes from American researcher Jacob Kounin. Watching teachers working with challenging classes, he notes that the difference between effective and ineffective teachers is not how they stop bad behaviour at the end of an escalating chain of events, but whether they are 'able to stop the chain before it started'. You can read a brief account of his work in Malcolm Gladwell's enjoyable book of essays, *What the Dog Saw* (Allen Lane, 2009).

This means that setting the climate for learning, having routines, making explicit your expectations and then being highly attuned to the emotional temperature of your classroom – all of these matter hugely.

Reliance on complicated systems of sanctions *after* bad behaviour has happened will rarely be as effective as pre-empting it.

Here is how to set clear expectations. Think of it like this: We should aim to:

1 set out our expectations clearly;

2 model the behaviour and language we expect from students.

In responding to challenging behaviour, we should:

3 give students choices, rather than box them into a corner;

4 avoid public confrontation, where necessary by being prepared to defer issues to the end of a lesson.

In practice, this means that:

1 *As teacher, you create the climate for behaviour*: the way you greet students, where you stand to speak to them, the seating plan, the air temperature, the pace, the sense of structure and order . . . all of these are important.

2   *Emotional feedback is the most powerful type*: smiles, 'well done', thumbs up, using names. It may be backed up by, say, stickers, comments in the homework diary, postcards home and so on, but make sure you do the one-to-one stuff first.

3   *Courtesy isn't an optional extra*: expect and model good manners – remind students about saying 'please' and 'thank you', holding doors open, listening to others. Create an ethos that is high on expectations of courtesy by being hugely courteous yourself.

4   *Lesson planning shapes students' behaviour*: the biggest impact on the group's behaviour will be the work you expect them to do – clear, varied activities, good pace, appropriate challenge, a strong emphasis on what students are expected to learn.

5   *Deal with misbehaviour calmly*: focus on the effect of the poor behaviour on others; give a choice ('Are you going to sit and work there quietly, or do you need to move over here?'); move the student if necessary; but don't have a public confrontation – defer it to the end of the lesson, when other students have left.

That sense of calm, recognisable and familiar routines matters a lot in good teaching. It is part of the teacher's craft.

As you train to teach and as you establish yourself as a new teacher, build routines that you stick to and that your students expect from you – for example:

- where you stand as they arrive;
- what you ask them to do as they arrive (coats off, bags off desks, books, planners and pens on tables, and suchlike);
- how you take the register (explicitly, publicly and in complete silence);
- how you kick-start the lesson;
- how you signal that it's time for a transition between one activity and the next;

- how you pull activities together at the end of the lesson, reviewing learning, giving praise, packing the class up in good time.

Undertaking these approaches in a consistent way in every lesson won't make you robotic. Quite the reverse, in fact: they will help you to exude confidence, reassuring students that they know what to expect from you, and then – biggest secret of all – they will liberate you to be creative in the parts of teaching that really matter: the pedagogy, the stuff of your subject.

It is the biggest secret in teaching – that consistency liberates creativity.

So be consistent. Get the basics nailed. And then you can be creative within a clearly established framework.

TALKING POINTS

- Does anything here surprise you or seem unrealistic?
- What kinds of routine will you give special emphasis to in your teaching?

WHAT I LOVE ABOUT TEACHING

Spending time teaching a subject I really love.
On a good day it feels a real privilege to do this.
In teaching the subject and having to explain it, I find I have become much more of an expert.

22 Using Teachers' Standard 8

Fulfil wider professional responsibilities

In some countries, the role of the teacher is to turn up, teach some lessons, mark books and then go home.

The expectation in the UK has always been deeper, with an emphasis on pastoral care, character building and the social, moral and cultural development of young people.

Although schools can sometimes feel like exam factories, in truth most pay considerable attention to developing our children into rounded individuals.

There's a feeling that we expect our education system to do more than produce a conveyor belt of effective students. We want other stuff to happen as well – such as music and drama and sport.

In his handy guide to the Teachers' Standards, one of the authors of them, Roy Blatchford, reminds us of a well-respected and much-quoted book from 1979, *Fifteen Thousand Hours: Secondary schools and their effects on children*. Written by Michael Rutter and a team of academics, it shone a light into the hidden curriculum of schools – the activities and interactions that happen outside and around the classroom. Its title arises from the telling statistic that, between the ages of five and sixteen, the average child will spend around 15,000 hours in school.

As a teacher, much of your time will, of course, be in the classroom, but this Standard is also concerned with your wider contribution to the school and the kind of impact you could make on some of those young people, during some of those 15,000 hours when they are not in lessons.

Here is what the Standards say:

Teachers should:

8(a) make a positive contribution to the wider life and ethos of the school;

8(b) develop effective professional relationships with colleagues, knowing how and when to draw on advice and specialist support;

8(c) deploy support staff effectively;

8(d) take responsibility for improving teaching through appropriate professional development, responding to advice and feedback from colleagues;

8(e) communicate effectively with parents with regard to pupils' achievements and well-being.

These expectations are what make schools rewarding places in which to work and what often enrich our role as a teacher. You will be making a contribution to the life of the school if you accompany or lead a school trip, or if you volunteer to coach a sports or debating team, or if you help with a fundraising event.

All such activities are likely to make school life more rewarding for you and will send out important messages to students about the importance of volunteering, about the way learning reaches beyond the confines of the classroom, about the pleasure of getting involved.

Experience tells us that those students who often gain most from life at school are those who take part in most, who pack their lunchtimes and after-school sessions with extra-curricular activities.

Many of us feel that something similar enriches our career as a teacher.

Notice that the Standards are expecting something else too. They talk of knowing how to deploy teaching assistants and other adults. This is an important skill, because, in schools where the adults are not thoughtfully deployed, it can be a wasted opportunity –

expensive and disappointing. You'll see this if you observe lessons where the teacher is talking to the class, and the teaching assistant is sitting at the back. It's usually not a good use of her time.

The skill, therefore, is in seeing a teaching assistant as a valuable additional resource to help some students learn faster and more effectively. This process is always better if you and she can liaise in advance, so that she knows what the lesson activity is and what the students are expected to learn.

A teaching assistant might draw up a separate handout or summary sheet to support students who might struggle with the main activity; she might work with an individual or small group of students inside your classroom; or she might take a small group of them outside to a new location, to help secure the students' skills and knowledge.

This is something learned through practice, rather than left to chance. If you have a regular teaching assistant in a lesson, make sure she feels centrally involved and that the two of you find time, however briefly, to plan the necessary interventions and then to evaluate their effectiveness.

Note also the expectation that you will participate in training and professional development. Gone is the era when teachers stayed for an occasional meeting to grind through information about new additions to the stock cupboard.

Training is no longer optional: it is a key part of the Standards, and quite right too. However, remember that the Standards are in part about providing evidence of your contribution to the wider life of the school, and so you will want to keep a portfolio or log of the training undertaken, perhaps with a brief reflection on what you feel you learned from it.

Finally, in this section, there is the contact with parents that forms part of the Standard. Most parents really appreciate being kept informed about the progress of their children. They love it – as do the students themselves – when a handwritten postcard or notelet drops through the letterbox, saying little more, perhaps, than 'well done'.

Teacher training

Do try to do this with a handwritten note rather than an email. It counts for such a lot. There are other links with parents, including attending parent consultation evenings and phone calls home when homework hasn't been handed in or there is another problem.

In the early stage of your career, talk to a colleague before making contact. Rehearse the kinds of point you want to make. Think of how best to say it. In my experience, something like this starts the process best:

> Hello, is that Mrs Stacey? It's Geoff Barton here from school. I'm Molly's English teacher and there's a small problem I need to discuss. Is now a convenient moment?

That mix of courtesy and formality usually works well. Occasionally, however, such interactions can go wrong, and we look at those later in this part.

How might you demonstrate that you are meeting the Standards?

This is a definite case for keeping a portfolio in which you keep examples of:

- training sessions attended;
- any extra-curricular activities and visits you have participated in;
- examples of planning or evaluations with a teaching assistant;
- notes or emails from students or parents thanking you for your help in dealing with a pastoral issue.

TALKING POINTS

- What problems do you foresee in maintaining a slim file of evidence for these Standards?
- Are there any parts of the advice you disagree with?

Using Part 2 of the Teachers' Standards

How to conduct yourself as a teacher – your personal and professional conduct

This section goes to the heart of what society should rightly expect from you as a teacher. Your role is one of considerable responsibility – you are placed in a position of trust and expected to ensure that students are safe as well as making the best progress possible.

The Teachers' Standards probably say everything that is needed on this important topic:

What the Standards say:

> Uphold public trust in the profession and maintain high standards of ethics and behaviour, within and outside school, by:
>
> (a) treating pupils with dignity, building relationships rooted in mutual respect, and at all times observing proper boundaries appropriate to a teacher's professional position;
>
> (b) having regard for the need to safeguard pupils' well-being, in accordance with statutory provisions;
>
> (c) showing tolerance of and respect for the rights of others;
>
> (d) not undermining fundamental British values, including democracy, the rule of law, individual liberty and mutual respect, and tolerance of those with different faiths and beliefs;

91

(e) ensuring that personal beliefs are not expressed in ways which exploit pupils' vulnerability or might lead them to break the law.

Have proper and professional regard for the ethos, policies and practices of the school in which they teach and maintain high standards in their own attendance and punctuality.

Have an understanding of, and always act within, the statutory frameworks which set out their professional duties and responsibilities.

Being a teacher does carry responsibilities not seen in many other jobs. Your conduct and your potential to bring the school into disrepute, or the risk you run of being targeted for complaints – all of these mean we have to be hypersensitive.

We have to be careful of how we behave, where we go, what we do. Going into town with friends, for example, and heading to pubs and clubs frequented by students encompasses a whole area that can lead, at the very least, to an uncomfortably self-conscious evening.

Even more, we need to protect ourselves online. Until a few years ago, self-protection was fairly straightforward – we could take responsibility for our conduct in school and outside school, often avoiding living and socialising in areas where we were likely to see and be seen by students. It was possible to compartmentalise our professional and private lives.

Social media have made that more difficult, and our sense of knowing how to police our online selves has become important.

If you use Facebook and similar social network sites, then privacy settings need very careful attention. Here's why:

At interview of all candidates hoping to gain a post at our school, I ask two important questions. The first is: 'You have written on your application form that you have no criminal record. Is that correct?'

I ask this so that the candidate has been asked to tell me the truth about his or her background. His answer, before an interview panel, will always be witnessed, and I make a written note of what he says. If it transpires that the candidate has not told the truth on the application and then in person, I have grounds for either not proceeding with the appointment or for subsequent dismissal.

So if you have any criminal offence that is going to show up in the mandatory Disclosure and Barring Service (DBS) checks (formerly Criminal Record Bureau (CRB)), then you need to put it on your application form and be ready to explain the circumstances at interview.

As a headteacher who presides over every teaching interview for new teachers at our school, I see a lot of such incidents. More often than not the offence was something that took place in the applicant's teenage years and involved alcohol or drugs or some form of driving offence.

I always ask candidates about what happened and watch their reaction.

If it's something that you feel might prevent you from being called to interview, then I would recommend that you refer to the incident in your letter and say that you would welcome an opportunity 'to discuss the issue at interview in order to explain why it will have no bearing on my role as a teacher'.

All of this will feel uncomfortable, but you are better being transparent and open about any such issue, rather than appearing to hide it. If you can show what you have learned from the experience and how it has helped to make you the person you are today, then so much the better.

There is a second question too: 'Is there anything in your private life that, if it came to the surface, would bring this school into disrepute?'

Candidates often go wide-eyed in panic at this point, as they scrabble around the corners of their memory to see if there is something they should mention. I therefore spell out what I'm talking about:

> If I look you up via Google will I find you on Facebook? Will I read your tweets? Will I find photographs of you in the past that you would rather I didn't see? Will I come across YouTube clips of you?

93

Teacher training

This is one reason why you need to be extremely cautious as a teacher, and as a would-be teacher, recognising that the nature of our profession makes the kind of social presence that your friends might enjoy impossible.

As someone who uses social media a lot, the way I look at it is this: before posting any comment, via Facebook or Twitter, I ask myself, 'Would I be happy for this to be printed on the front page of the *Daily Mail*?' That means I won't post anything that reveals anything about my family life, about alcohol or about sexual issues, or that uses bad language. If in doubt about the content of a post, I won't go ahead.

This form of self-regulation is essential if you are to enjoy a career in which you minimise the risk of being accused of unprofessional conduct.

It is no longer enough to maintain professional standards through how you dress, talk and behave in school. Those expectations extend to your online self: police it with great caution.

TALKING POINTS

- Is there anything online now that could cause you embarrassment?
- Are you sure?
- If so, what will you do about it now?

---

24 How to use language as a teacher

This title isn't necessarily as daft as it seems.

Language is a teacher's bread and butter. It is what we use. Watch a great teacher of Mathematics at work and what you'll see is the clever use of explanation, of questioning, of not always giving an answer, of pausing, using silence, lifting an eyebrow.

Skilfully using language – spoken language and body language – is fundamental to becoming a great teacher. That's why it deserves more attention from the very start of our careers, from our earliest training onwards.

Partly that's because it is during our earliest time as teachers that bad habits can set in. Unless we have someone critiquing our work periodically, or put ourselves through the self-conscious process of recording and listening back to ourselves, then it is easy for certain mannerisms, certain words and phrases, to lodge themselves in our way of speaking.

That is why, right at the start of becoming a teacher, it is worth looking at how to talk as a teacher – that is, how to use language effectively.

Insist on silence

One of the main differences between a lesson taught by an expert teacher and one taught by a newcomer is that the expert will insist on – absolutely demand – silence when he or she is speaking.

Teacher training

This arises from a kind of inner confidence, a self-belief that is – of course – a bit of a con-trick. It is built on the assumption that when I, as the main adult in the classroom, speak, then you, the class of students, must listen.

Without this unwritten agreement between teacher and students, high-quality learning is very unlikely to happen. So, from the very start, insist on silence. Many of us do this by having a trigger phrase or two, essentially saying to students, 'Listen to me'.

What you don't want to do is to raise your voice to gain the attention of the class. There is little that is more unbecoming, and sometimes painfully humiliating to witness, than a fledgling or veteran teacher who is working harder and harder in beseeching the class to be quiet.

That is why many of us use phrases such as, 'Thank you. Pens down and everyone looking this way'.

There are a couple of points to note here. First, 'thank you' is a more powerful than 'please'. It is built on the assumption that you will do what I say, rather than require me to plead with you. Make 'thank you' part of your verbal repertoire.

Note also the physical expectation of stillness that is required in the 'pens down' command. We know that there is no logical reason that students cannot hold a pen and listen perfectly well, but the phrase requires them to do something and then gives you, as teacher, a clear visual clue about who is listening.

If you are softly spoken, you might clap your hands to gain attention as you say the phrase. I sometimes tap some keys or a board rubber on the desk. I have – as I'm recommending you should have – some familiar and repeatable cues to students that it is time for them to be still and listen in silence.

Then, you need to insist on it, so if someone at the side of the room hasn't put her pen down, look at her until she does, or say 'Pen down, please' or – raising the stakes slightly with a question – 'Did you hear me ask for pens down and looking this way?'

You will want to develop your own verbal and visual cues. They will be an essential part of the process of developing your air of authority in the classroom, making it easier to draw the class back to full attention, to explain things, to move the lesson on. So be ruthless on this one: insist on silence.

Ask better questions

Teachers ask a lot of questions, usually requiring answers that we already know ourselves. It is one of the more surreal aspects of how teachers use language – unlike in the real world out there, our questions aren't usually designed to find out things that we don't know; they're to find out whether our students know what we know.

High quality questions are an important feature of high quality teaching. That means thinking about the purpose of the questions you ask, thinking whether there might be other ways of getting a wider range of students in the class to demonstrate their knowledge, rather than the one who directly answers your question.

I suggest the following elements will improve your questioning skills.

First, create a culture in which questions aren't just the age-old ritual of a teacher asking something, a few familiar hands going up, and the same student enthusiasts dutifully parroting their answer, while the rest of the class listens passively, or doesn't.

A culture for better questioning will arise if you can do two things.

First, try to break the tyranny of students putting their hands up. Develop a sense that anyone in the room can be asked to give an answer, that there's no need to put up a hand. This often sounds counter-intuitive to teachers who haven't seen it in action, and it can be perceived as unnerving for students, who may not know what to say and, therefore, leave embarrassing, unwanted silences.

That is why, second, together with the no-hands-up approach, you must build in student thinking time, or 'oral rehearsal'. Thinking time means saying to students:

97

Teacher training

> I'm going to ask some people to explain to me why earthquakes happen. I'm looking for two or three main reasons based on what we've been studying. Have one minute to think what you're going to say and then I'll choose some people.

Oral rehearsal means giving students that minute or so – no more – to rehearse their answer with a partner. This builds their confidence, gets over some self-consciousness issues and can lead to better-expressed answers.

These two approaches will begin to create a culture in which all students know that your questions are designed for all to answer, rather than just the keenies.

That is where you need to ask better questions. These will more often than not be 'how?' and 'why?' questions, rather than 'what?'.

'What?' questions are fine for recalling basic knowledge, for checking students know facts and theories, but it is the 'how?' and 'why?' questions that take them deeper, that lead to exploration of processes, that lead us further into students having the skills to apply, analyse, synthesise and evaluate.

That is where, from the outset, we should plan our questions: if we are clear about what skills and knowledge we want our students to demonstrate, then we will get better, deeper answers from better questioning, probably through fewer questions than the old scattergun approach led to, supported by a culture of no hands up, thinking time and oral rehearsal.

One other thing: don't accept the first good answer you get from a student. In fact, try to comment less on answers than teachers traditionally have. It is all too easy for us to ask a question, choose someone with their hand up, listen to their answer, say 'good answer' and then move on.

If one student is answering a question, we can't know whether other students are also understanding to the same degree.

So develop a repertoire in response to students' answers. Rather than accept the first response you get, make it part of the Q&A culture of your classroom that students know that you are likely to ask someone else for their answer, and then someone else; and then to ask someone else to comment on which of the three answers so far he most agrees with and why; and then to do the same with another student.

Thus, questioning becomes a core activity in which we work as a group to explore issues, to deepen our collective understanding, to make judgements about what has been said and to explore how we might express our learning better.

Questioning in this way is perhaps the most important skill we have as teachers – it is a type of human interaction that other forms of learning (e.g. on line) seem unlikely to replicate. So use every opportunity to develop your questioning skills and, when possible, get to watch other teachers – good or bad – at work.

All of it will help you, through practice and reflection, to become a better questioner and, what follows from it, a better teacher.

Explain more effectively

This is an underrated part of what we have to do as teachers. We have to explain stuff. Whether it is giving an account of something in our subject – 'here's why the Periodic Table matters' – or describing how today's lesson will unfold, we spend a lot of time explaining.

Experience suggests that clear, understandable explanations are essential. Too often, what students complain of is teachers who talk too much or repeat too much or go into too much detail.

Learning to explain with clarity and flair is essential. It is also the way that you will show students how to use vocabulary that is essential for their subject. You will show them how to speak like a scientist, historian or musician. It is one of the most important responsibilities you have.

Here is how to do it. First, know what you want to say. Give students the outline, but, if there is additional detail, you might have that on the whiteboard and simply refer them to it. There are times when it is quite right that you should talk a lot, especially as the expert in the room.

Teacher training

However, explanations usually benefit from being concise and providing an overarching, understandable shape to what students need to take in.

That's where being redundant rather than repetitive in your speech makes a difference. Redundancy is a term from linguistics and (in this case) from rhetoric. Here is how a Wikipedia entry explains it (perfectly): 'Through the use of repetition of certain concepts, redundancy increases the odds of predictability of a message's meaning and understanding to others'.

That is precisely what I am recommending – that you deploy key words and phrases redundantly to add clarity to your explanations and instructions. That is not the same as repeating information that you have already mentioned.

So an explanation about how students are expected to approach a task might sound like this:

> We've been studying Elizabethan England for a few lessons now. Today it's time for you to demonstrate to me what you have learned. You're going to do this in three ways.
>
> First, you're going to work in a three to decide what the key ideas of the period are. You'll present these on a one-screen poster or PowerPoint page.
>
> Second, you'll think about how to present this knowledge to the rest of the group in a two-minute 'speed dating' exercise. There are more details about what's required in this second task here on the board.
>
> Finally, you'll be visiting each other group and absorbing their information as quickly as possible, ready to demonstrate to me in the last twenty minutes that you have become experts in this period.
>
> So there are three main tasks you'll need to do, and just forty minutes to work through them.

As ever, an outline of teacher speech like this feels phoney when written out on the page. Let's accept that. But it does illustrate the way in which connectives ('first, second, finally') are being used to help structure the explanation in students' minds. It uses words such as 'this' and 'here' to draw attention to additional information. It uses the classic 'rule of three' to organise the sequence of activities and bring clarity.

There is one other essential ingredient in effective explanations: using metaphor. Great teachers can take complex subjects and render them simple, but not too simple. They can help students to understand processes that initially baffle them.

Metaphor is when we compare one thing with another. We get students to visualise something abstract or unseen (molecules) and use language that helps them to visualise what might be happening ('dancing', 'bumping into each other', 'bouncing faster and faster').

It is worth watching some great teachers at work in, say, Physics or Chemistry or History, watching the way they are able to help their students to absorb the essential essence of concepts and processes by their ability to make analogies and tell stories. Being able to do so will make your own explanations clearer and more powerful.

Read aloud well

There will be times when you need to read aloud from a textbook or handout or article. Do this well. Model to students what good reading aloud sounds like and how we use the structure and punctuation in texts to help us understand them.

Here are some hints:

- Don't get students reading a text aloud unless you have given them preparation time: it can undermine their confidence in reading publicly. Instead, you read.

- Make sure you have read the text through in advance, so that you are familiar with it: this will save you getting tangled on any parts that are obscurely expressed or badly phrased.

Teacher training

- Use the punctuation to guide your reading: pause at commas and full stops for slightly longer than you might expect to. Overall, read a bit more slowly than feels natural.

- Insist that students follow the text as you read – have it on a screen at the front of the room, or in front of each one. In this way, they get to see how confident readers (that is, you!) read texts, how we use intonation, and how we use punctuation to demarcate units of meaning.

- Seize any opportunity you can to make explicit to students how you read, decode and interpret a text – like this:

Before reading:

> So before I read the text I look at the title. I make a prediction about what the article might be about. I also try to work out how reliable this text will be – is it by an author I know of? Is it in a publication that's trustworthy? How can I tell? Knowing these things will help me as I read to know whether to trust exactly what is being said, or whether I should be more cautious about it.

During reading:

> I've paused at this word because it's one that I don't know – or at least I'm not confident that I know it. So I'm wondering which words it reminds me of – are there words with a similar start ('photo-')? Can I use them to help me to work out what the meaning of this word is? Does the context (plants and light) help? Has the writer included a glossary at the end of the article that I can refer to, or does the next sentence help me to work out the meaning more clearly?

After reading:

> So, I think a bit about what the article is saying. I try to sum up its main points. I could do this in three or four bullet

points, or in a spider diagram. What I'm trying to do is to make sure that I have fully grasped what the writer has said.

My next job is to think about how he has said it. That's going to let me move on to higher skills – deciding whether I agree with the writer, whether this is a text I should trust or dispute.

In reading aloud well, and in commenting on what you do before, during and after reading, you perform one of the most important acts a teacher can do – initiating those students for whom reading is often an alien, unfathomable process and bringing them into the domain of the literate. You help them, in other words, to see why the ability to read well is so central to being able to learn well. You demystify the mysterious.

Don't underestimate language

If you have read the preceding advice and thought anything from 'not relevant to me' to 'he's a literacy nutter', stop now. Language is how we communicate. It is how we understand one another. In schools and colleges, it is how we pass on knowledge and skills from one generation to the next. It is how we help students to understand ideas, to develop their intellect, to build their social skills, to refine how to be human.

Language is what defines us. So don't underestimate its importance in class.

Experience tells me that, if a teacher of Mathematics or Design Technology or Science or English isn't much good, language is often near the heart of the issue.

Whether it is that we are not explaining well enough, or asking too many questions, or simply talking too much – language can have a huge effect on reducing our power as teachers.

So make it an ongoing priority to think about language, to use it well and to monitor what you are doing with it.

In particular, be attuned to the dreadful, irksome language traits that we can all pick up. These are the mannerisms that we notice in other staff when they lead assemblies, or we hear in colleagues at staff meetings, or in students when they speak in class.

They are the fillers and the repetitions and the clichés – the 'likes', the 'okays' the 'you know what I means'.

Just as we need, from time to time, to purge our hard drives and reboot our servers, so we need to be mindful of our own speech habits. Irritating and unnecessary verbal mannerisms can set in and, if we don't notice them ourselves, they can harden and fester.

So, as the final message of this chapter, regularly pay attention to the way you use language – whether it involves you asking a colleague to observe you and give feedback, or (wincingly) recording your own lesson on video or audio, or using student evaluation that asks for open feedback on your teaching style.

All of this will make you a much better teacher.

TALKING POINTS

- Which aspects of this unit do you need to think more about?
- Which other teachers have you observed and admired or winced at?
- What verbal mannerisms are you already conscious of developing?

25 How to use classroom routines to establish good behaviour as the norm

Creating and maintaining a calm, orderly ethos is important. Effective learning can rarely take place without it.

It is easy to overcomplicate the management of behaviour using systems designed to reward students' good behaviour, to deter them from behaving badly and to punish them if they transgress.

All schools are likely to have something at the heart of their ethos that is designed to do this. At the very least, the school will want to encourage students to do things that are nice rather than nasty.

However, especially as new teachers, we can become fixated on these systems, thinking that they are the key to good behaviour.

In reality, students will behave well because they see the relevance of what they are doing, or because they like it, or because some other, intangible reward for doing it motivates them.

That is where classroom routines are important in setting the tone for behaviour, in establishing a culture from which positive, courteous behaviour arises, almost unthinkingly.

Here are some ground rules.

In general, as stated earlier, we should aim to:

- set out our expectations clearly;
- model the behaviour and language we expect from students.

Teacher training

For the majority of our students, for most of the time, this approach, consistently applied, will suffice. Good behaviour from most members of our classes will follow.

If, however, you have to respond to poor behaviour, you should:

- Give students choices, rather than box them into a corner.
- Avoid public confrontation, where necessary, by being prepared to defer issues to the end of a lesson.

Setting the tone for behaviour means using a series of routines and sticking to these every lesson. Here is what I would recommend:

At the start of lessons:

- Try to be in the room before students arrive, standing at the door as they come in.
- Ensure that coats have been taken off, books and equipment are quickly taken out, and bags are placed on the floor; planners or homework diaries should be on students' desks.
- Aim to take a register within the first ten minutes of the lesson (even if not formally, by calling out names, it is important that students *know* that the register is nevertheless being taken).
- Make the learning objectives clear, and return to them at the end of the lesson.

When dealing with lateness:

- Never ignore lateness. You mustn't be seen to condone it. Politely ask any late students why they are late, and then decide quickly whether this is an acceptable explanation. (One acceptable reason for several students arriving late might, for example, be that this morning's assembly overran.) If there isn't an acceptable reason, don't provoke a public row: simply say that you will want to see the late students at the end of the lesson when the others leave. Then, for a first offence, make a point of writing (slowly) in the student's planner that he or she arrived late. This means that the parent and tutor should see the note. You, meanwhile, have inconvenienced the student by keeping him or her back to make the note and signalled to other, prompt, students that you won't turn a blind eye to lateness.

Using praise:

- Aim to praise students as much as possible, but make it meaningful praise – that is, commenting on things that matter.

- Praise might include: saying 'well done', issuing a merit sticker or some other device advocated in the school's behaviour code or making a note in the planner.

- Of all of these, saying 'well done' (or words to that effect) is probably the most important.

Dealing with disruption:

- Make it clear to a misbehaving student how this is affecting the class (that is, focus on the misdemeanour, not the person).

- Ask the student whether she would prefer to move to sit nearer to you rather than stay where she currently is.

- If necessary, move the student.

- If behaviour problems persist, defer the matter to the end of the lesson and deal with the issue in private. Unless it is very significant, you are far better tackling such concerns without an audience of curious students.

Finishing lessons:

- Build in time for students to review what they have learned, referring back to the learning objectives; write homework on the board and ensure that it is copied into the planner; check that students have done this by walking around the room, looking at planners.

Teacher training

- Expect students to pack away quietly, tidying the furniture (chairs on desks at the end of the day) and picking up any residual litter; leave the board clean.

- Dismiss the quietest row/groups first (rather than all at once, or by gender), preferably standing at the door as they leave.

  Establish classroom routines:

- Arrive at the room before students arrive and get the register ready; stand at the door as the students come in.

- Leave the door to the classroom open for five minutes; any students arriving after this time are officially late and should hand you their planner; see these students at the end of the lesson, having made a note in the 'comments' section that they were late to your lesson; their tutor and parents will then become aware; also record the late and any comments on the register.

- Consciously decide upon and plan the seating arrangements for students, rather than leaving them to decide where they wish to sit; make it clear every lesson that the decision about where students sit is yours; help yourself by moving students around frequently; keep reinforcing the fact that this is your territory.

- Ensure that coats have been taken off, books and equipment are quickly taken out, and bags are placed on the floor; planners should be on students' desks.

- Take a register within the first few minutes of the lesson; do this publicly – for example, by calling students names out while they sit in silence; this reinforces their awareness that attendance is being checked.

- Make the learning objectives clear – or whatever formulation you use of what students will learn this lesson – usually by having them on display, and return to them at the end of the lesson.

- Aim to praise students as much as possible, formally and informally.

- Give thinking time after asking a question (e.g. 'Have five seconds to think what your answer is'); this will lead to far better answers.

- Ask fewer questions, using more open-ended styles of question ('Explain to me *how/why* this happens . . .'; 'What are the three main ingredients in this process . . .?'; 'How do we know what the author thinks . . .?').

- Limit the use of putting hands up (whereby the same small number of students often answer most of the questions); instead, say, 'Discuss what your answer will be for thirty seconds, then I'll ask people to tell me – no need to put hands up'.

- Promote active student participation in learning, with them leading starters and plenaries, chairing meetings, giving feedback on each other's performances, and so on.

- Make it clear to a misbehaving student how this is affecting the class (focusing on the misdemeanour, not the person).

When a student is disrupting or disturbing others, you might:

- stop teaching and wait for them to calm down;
- have a quiet word about the need to behave;
- ask them to stop the disruption;
- move them to a different seat;
- in exceptional circumstances (such as serious defiance), call for support from another member of staff.

Teacher training

TALKING POINTS

- There is a lot here to assimilate: which parts do you most agree with? Which are you less certain of?
- What kinds of routine will become part of your repertoire to give students a consistent set of expectations of your teaching?

26 How to emphasise your classroom expectations

Routines matter a lot, as we have seen. They liberate rather than suppress creativity.

Sometimes, it is useful to have on display somewhere a set of expectations. Occasionally – just occasionally – it is going to be necessary to remind students of these, especially if they are losing interest, becoming restless or becoming sloppy in their attitudes.

It's not that you will ask students to write out these expectations. Instead, like so many aspects of teaching, they are there for symbolic reasons – as a visible reminder of what you expect from the students and what they should be able to expect from you and each other.

Here's a summary of what students should expect from you. It may be that you want a simple, easy-to-read summary like this clearly on display in your classroom, so that, when necessary, you can refer to it:

Start of lessons

- Quietly enter the room after I have arrived: I will always aim to be in the room before you. If I am not, please wait quietly outside in the corridor.

- Put your planner and equipment for the lesson on your desk, so that we can quickly get started.

Teacher training

- Listen carefully and follow instructions.
- Most importantly – be polite, be kind, be open-minded.

During lessons

- Remember that I will decide on seating arrangements and will regularly change groupings.
- I will aim to provide you with a range of activities to develop your understanding.
- If you don't understand something, ask – you won't get laughed at or humiliated because you haven't yet 'got' something. Real learning involves getting stuck.
- Listen to whoever is speaking without interrupting.
- Always be polite and respect others.
- You may drink water in class (no other drinks), provided there is not a health and safety risk.
- Bring me your planner if you need permission to leave the room. I'll need to make a note of what time you left.

End of lessons

- You will be asked to review and reflect on what you have learned.
- Take down homework instructions or write in 'None set'.
- Pack away and wait to be dismissed.
- Please leave the room neat and tidy.

TALKING POINTS

- Lists like these can come across as babyish or patronising. How do you respond to this?
- How would you customise it to reflect the expectations of your classroom?

WHAT I DISLIKE ABOUT TEACHING

The constant talk of Ofsted. Even after we had been inspected (and did all right as a school), Ofsted was still endlessly mentioned and frequently used to justify things we should be doing or not doing. I think there should be a ban on mentioning Ofsted.

27 How to use your body language to reinforce your expectations of good behaviour

This is the stuff no one ever told me when I was training to teach. I now know, from watching thousands of lessons in hundreds of classrooms, that it is not just what teachers know or what they say that matters. It is where they stand and how they stand. It is how they use gesture and how they don't use gesture.

These are all what we might call the micro-skills of teaching – the physical nitty-gritty that demonstrates implicitly to a class that the territory of the classroom is yours, that you set the expectations in here.

Here is how body language, stance, gesture and voice help to reinforce that sense of unspoken authority.

Table 27.1 What effective teachers do

Where to stand	• Avoid allowing 'no-go zones' to develop by standing in different places – e.g. reading aloud from a point at the back or distant edge of a classroom. This signals that all parts of this classroom belong to you
	• Circulate around the classroom
	• Address the class from a position of authority – in particular, avoid having a barrier (e.g. a desk) between yourself and the class
	• Move students to different locations for different activities and lessons: use the classroom creatively and on your own terms

How to stand	• Stand still
	• Reinforce your authority by waiting until the class is silent before speaking. Absolutely insist upon this
	• Move around when reading, often choosing a position behind the students
Use of body language	• Smile, frown, stare, as necessary: don't subscribe to the 'Don't smile till Christmas' mantra
	• Use commanding gestures – clear arm movements, rhetorical flourishes, pointing, gestures for emphasis
Use of eye contact	• Sweep the class with your eyes: every student needs to feel that you routinely look at him or her
	• Use a glance to stop someone from losing concentration
	• Look students in the eye
	• Avoid having papers or notes as a barrier between you and the class
Use of voice	• Wait before speaking
	• Avoid repetition of verbal fillers ('okay', 'know what I mean', 'right')
	• Be clearly audible but . . . . . . use texture of volume – some bits loud, some bits quiet
	• Use students' names a lot
	• Say 'thank you' more than 'please' (this adds to your authority: it is based on an assumption that students will do things, rather than your having to plead with them to do so)
	• Don't talk too much – doing so is one of the biggest catalysts to students losing interest and going off task.
	• Explain clearly, ask whether students need clarification, and then shut up
	• Have alternatives to asking questions – different ways that students can show they have learned things, rather than you asking a question, and one student at a time responding
	• Ask 'why?' and 'how?' more than 'what?' – as this approach beds in, you'll get deeper answers
	• Give thinking time before expecting answers

Teacher training

Use of silence	• Pause longer than a class might expect
	• Wait for, and insist on, silence
	• Give thinking time after a question
Use of praise and feedback	• Praise hugely and in a varied way – well done, 'nice one', 'great idea', 'fabulous', 'hadn't thought of that'
Social dynamics (the hardest one to pin down)	• Hit the ground running at the start of a lesson
	• Change direction to suit the group
	• Make jokes, but do more than entertain
	• Know when to say 'enough is enough'
	• Become respected and popular with students, but don't simply court popularity: your friends are outside the classroom, not within it
Clarity of explanations	• Explain work in a clear but non-patronising way
	• Allow students to raise issues of concern and respond with concise and confident answers

---

TALKING POINTS

- How do you know where to stand when you teach?
- Do you instinctively use a range of locations?
- Have you thought about how to avoid the build-up of 'no-go zones' in the classroom?
- What might you try doing more of or less of as a result of this list?

WHAT I LOVE ABOUT TEACHING

There is something new every day. Of course, this can be exhausting, and sometimes you feel there are too many things to think about. But overall the variety in this job is amazingly rewarding.

28 How to deal with challenging behaviour

Part A: exploring the issues

You will enhance your skills in dealing with the whole range of behaviour – from exemplary to terrible – by actively learning from others. Watch some of the veterans of the staffroom. Watch those who use techniques rather than charisma or long-serving reputation to gain students' respect. Note their deployment of that elusive skill 'withitness' in knowing when to intervene, when to pause, when to say something mild, when to ignore.

All of this is what great teachers do, and it helps if they have established themselves as consistent in the classroom.

That's where routines matter so much, so that the student grapevine characterises you as fair but firm, approachable but consistent.

You will also significantly enhance your reputation about school if you see break or lunchtime or after-school duty as an integral part of the teacher's job. That doesn't mean that you have to go on duty all the time, but instead understand that this is one of those core parts of our work that contributes to the school's ethos – keeping the place calm and reassuring, however grim the weather.

It is also when students will imperceptibly be gaining impressions of you.

That is why I always encourage trainee teachers to spend time with an established member of staff on break or lunch or bus duty. Watch how an informal word, a snatched conversation, a word of rebuke or praise can feed into the perception that this teacher is someone who is a reassuring authority figure around school.

That is what you will want to be.

There are a few simple tips for establishing yourself like that, but watching and being seen to be out there, rather than skulking in an office, can only enhance your reputation among students. It goes with the teaching territory, and, as you gain confidence, you will enjoy being in the corridor, or at the back gate, or in the canteen, and you will use it as a relentless opportunity to network with students.

That said, there will be times when you face challenging behaviour. We all do. In a school of perhaps a thousand teenagers, their moods and hormones sloshing about wildly, we should not be surprised if sometimes interactions go awry.

Take a look at these five 'behaviour dilemmas'. Think about how you might react to them. Then read the notes that follow. These aren't being presented as a simplistic tick list of 'what to do if . . .'. Behaviour issues will rarely be as easily characterised as that. Instead, they are thoughts on what you might do, or might have done, to minimise the impact of challenging behaviour.

- Behaviour Dilemma 1: You are walking along behind a group of Year 10 students. One of them throws an empty soft drink can on the path. What do you do?

- Behaviour Dilemma 2: You have been asked at the last minute to cover a lesson. The class is already in the room and being boisterous. You can't immediately see the work that has been set. What do you do?

- Behaviour Dilemma 3: A girl in your tutor group is wearing trainers in a school that insists that students wear shoes. She has a reputation for being quite fiery. You feel it is important that she conforms to uniform policy. What do you do?

- Behaviour Dilemma 4: You are teaching your subject, and a boy keeps talking to his friend. When you ask him why he isn't working, he says the work is 'boring'. What do you do?

- Behaviour Dilemma 5: You are teaching a Year 10 class and hear Student X call Student Y an 'ugly slag'. Student Y overhears this and complains, asking you to do something. Student X starts denying it. What do you do?

Think about the dilemmas yourself before reading the notes that follow.

TALKING POINTS

For each dilemma consider:
- Is there anything you could have done before this incident occurred to prevent it?
- Is it one to turn a strategic blind eye to?
- What do you do now?

ADVICE FOR NEW TEACHERS

Do as much preparation as possible during the holidays. In fact, have a plan for how to use your holidays. I like to get some work done at the start, before I can truly unwind anyway. Then I switch off and do no work. Then, as the back-to-school nerves kick in, I make life as easy for myself as possible by getting remaining preparation and marking done.

How to deal with challenging behaviour

Part B: some possible responses

Read this chapter with care. It is not a simple template that suggests 'if you do this, then the student will do that'. Life isn't quite as simple as those of us writing books and dishing out advice sometimes suggest.

It's messier.

So this isn't exactly a chapter of solutions. In fact, most issues relating to behaviour, especially challenging behaviour, don't have 'solutions' that are ready-made, neat and guaranteed.

Instead, there are simply some things we might do that are more likely to mean that we are successful, things that might just, in some circumstances, mean that the students modify their behaviour in the present and learn from their mistake for the future.

That, if achieved, is a perfect result.

Here's a commentary on the behaviour dilemmas:

BEHAVIOUR DILEMMA 1

Situation

You are walking along behind a group of Year 10 students.
One of them throws an empty soft-drink can on the path.
What do you do?

Response

You can't ignore this. It is too easy to turn a blind eye to inappropriate and bad behaviour when it happens outside the confines of your own classroom. However, you can't – because it is the stuff that happens between classrooms, around corridors, in the canteen and on the school field that shapes a school's ethos – what it feels like, how it expresses its values, how it reinforces its expectations.

A student throwing litter like this, ostentatiously and with disregard for common manners, must be challenged. So you'll say something like: 'Excuse me – can you just grab that can and put it in the bin over there? Thank you.'

Your 'excuse me' shows your own courtesy, rather than something confrontational.

BEHAVIOUR DILEMMA 2

Situation

You have been asked at the last minute to cover a lesson. The class is already in the room and being boisterous. You can't immediately see the work that has been set. What do you do?

Response

Covering a lesson is something that teachers are required to do less and less. Quite right too – it was always something that blighted the job, taking us away from planning and marking and not necessarily providing a good educational experience to students who were without their regular teacher.

However, cover did do something useful: it helped us to cut our teeth on the essential skills of the classroom. There was something about the need to take a class we didn't know and cover a subject we didn't know. It enabled some of us to develop various strategies for behaviour management, questioning and other core skills, and to do so in a context that, although it could be terrifying at first, did end up getting us to see other classrooms, in other subjects.

The answer here, I would suggest, is to find out what work has been set, as soon as you learn that you have been called to cover an absent colleague. Don't leave it until you arrive at the classroom. You don't want to have a group of up to thirty students asking you what they're doing, where their normal teacher is, whether they can just watch a video and what your name is while you are scrambling to try and find the work.

So get hold of the work first. It might be in a central location, such as the staffroom, or you might need to check whether it has been left, clearly labelled, on the absent teacher's desk.

Whatever you do, find the work, look to see that there is enough of it and that it feels appropriate (you don't want to have an hour in which students have only been given a word search).

I would also strongly suggest making contact with the head of department for the subject, asking about the work and whether she will be coming in to start the lesson. If so, that will help, because she will be able to explain the work to the class and take any specialist questions from them.

However, the dilemma is meaner than that: it suggests you arrive at the room, and there is no work. You haven't had a chance to do the preparatory work and now you simply need to cope.

Here is what I recommend:

Seize the territory. If the class is already in the room, you need to signal that it is now yours. Do this through some short, clear, polite instructions that essentially show that the expectations are all being set by you. Ask someone to open a window slightly. Ask for all bags to be off desks, all coats off, planners ready, pens down, everyone looking this way . . . all of this is the stuff teachers do to emphasise their authority.

That doesn't mean saying any of it aggressively. Just be firm.

Do two other things: immediately send a student to find the head of department or someone else nearby who is likely to be able to sort out the lack of work.

Then, having shown that you are now commanding the territory of the room (change the lighting slightly, take a deep breath, stand in the position that gives you greatest authority – i.e. not skulking behind the teacher's desk), speak. Expect students to be quiet. This is where your absolute self-belief is needed. So go for it – clap your hands, or tap the desk, or just say, 'Right, thank you, attention this way', or whatever suits your own emerging style for gaining attention.

Insist on silence. Insist on pens being down, on bags being off the tables, on all eyes looking your way. Insist on this. If there is someone still holding a pen, say, 'Pen down, thanks'.

All of this is symbolic, of course. It is establishing your authority, ready for the rest of the lesson.

Now, while waiting for the student 'runner' to return with work from the head of department, introduce yourself, say that you will be overseeing the lesson today and that you are just waiting for the work to arrive. Ask students to think about the topic they have most recently been working on with their regular teacher. Let's imagine that it is the history of medicine.

Say to students something like this:

> Okay – the history of medicine. As you know, I'm not a History teacher, so I don't know a lot about that topic. But you've been studying it, so you ought to. I'm going to give you three minutes with a partner to come up with the five essential points I should know about the history of medicine. You can write your points down.
>
> Then, when you've had your three minutes, I'm going to ask some people to tell me what their five main points are.

> No hands up: I'm just going to ask different people to give me their points. Then I'm going to ask someone else to tell me which two points that they have heard are the most important to understanding this topic.
>
> And then I'm going to ask you some questions about the topic, so that, as a group, you can demonstrate what you know and explain it to me.
>
> All right? So you have three minutes with your neighbour to come up with your five essential pieces of knowledge about the history of medicine. Start now.
>
> This buys you time and establishes your authority with the group, so that someone in the department – possibly the teacher next door – can come and set the 'official work'.
>
> In the meantime, you will have played a useful role in reinforcing the group's knowledge and in establishing yourself in the eyes of the group as a teacher who is calm, firm and fair and carries a sense of authority.

BEHAVIOUR DILEMMA 3

Situation

A girl in your tutor group is wearing trainers in a school that insists that students wear shoes. She has a reputation for being quite fiery. You feel it is important that she conforms to uniform policy. What do you do?

Response

This is another one that you cannot ignore. Just don't provoke a public confrontation. As soon as you notice the trainers, you need to ask why she is wearing trainers and where her normal shoes are. If they are in her bag, ask her to put them on. If she lives up to her reputation for fieriness and refuses and is defiant, defuse the situation by saying something like this:

> All right, I asked you very reasonably to take off the trainers and put on the shoes. You've refused. I'm not going to have a huge confrontation about it here and now, because that will distract everyone else. But I will follow the issue up at the end of the lesson.

Stay calm. Don't respond to any provocation. Ask her to stay behind at the end of the lesson. Go over what you have quite reasonably asked of her and say that you are informing both her tutor and head of year. Say you're disappointed that she defied you.

Then, let her go, and do what you said – inform her tutor and head of year that she was flouting school rules and defied you when you enforced them.

Then, try not to let the issue gnaw away at you or fester.

BEHAVIOUR DILEMMA 4

Situation

You are teaching your subject, and a boy keeps talking to his friend. When you ask him why he isn't working, he says the work is 'boring'. What do you do?

Response

Don't have a public confrontation. That might be precisely what the student is after.

I would suggest not saying much about the 'boring' comment. Instead, focus on the distracting nature of the background chatter and give the student a choice. He can either stay sitting where he is but needs to stop talking, or he can move to a seat nearer to your desk at the front of the room. Ask him which it is to be.

The good thing about this response is that you don't get mired in some childish discussion about what is boring and what is not. Instead, you keep the focus on the effect of the behaviour, which is likely to be distracting other students.

In your response, therefore, you have claimed the moral high ground (implicitly – there is no need to spell this out) of taking action on behalf of others in the group who want to be able to concentrate.

BEHAVIOUR DILEMMA 5

Situation

You are teaching a Year 10 class, and Student X apparently calls Student Y an 'ugly slag'. Student Y overhears this and complains, asking you to do something. You didn't hear the remark. When asked, Student X starts denying it. What do you do?

Response

This is another one that cannot be ignored, but, if it wasn't a public comment, then it's not something that needs a public response.

It is one to defer to the end of the lesson by saying that you want to see both students at that time to sort out what was said. If the issue is going to keep brewing, then you might need to move both the students – or at least to threaten to move both of them, giving them a choice as to whether they can work in silence until the end of the lesson or need both to be moved.

Moving both would be important, because it shows that you aren't judging Student X to have done something wrong without investigating.

Then, at the end of the lesson, give each student time to explain what happened. Whether you think that the offending phrase was used or not, you ought to pass a quick summary of the incident to the head of year and tutor, as there might be a history of such verbal abuse. In fact, there might be nastier behaviour going on.

You will definitely need to be guided on responding to this incident by your school's behaviour policy. If that demands a detention, then that is what should happen. Even if you can defuse the confrontation and restore the situation so that it seems harmonious, you need also to be seen to implement the 'official' sanctions. School consistency on discipline gets undermined when teachers and others start to do their own thing.

In terms of punishment, you will want, at the very least, for there to be some kind of apology and a guarantee that there won't be a repetition of the behaviour.

That said, it might be that a much sterner response is needed: if the lesson was disrupted, and other students were drawn in, then a detention might be the right response.

The main aims should be: to demonstrate that you don't turn a blind eye, but nor do you leap to conclusions about who has done what; to show that you will tackle issues, but you will do so in a calm, dispassionate manner; and to affirm constantly that yours is a classroom where only civilised behaviour will be allowed – anything else will be followed up.

Teacher training

TALKING POINTS

- Which of these dilemmas would you find the toughest to deal with?
- What do you think about the advice given? Which bits feel most right to you?
- Which parts do you disagree with?

WHAT I LOVE ABOUT TEACHING

Strangely enough, although I don't like all the marking I have to do, when the students produce amazing pieces of work you can get a real kick from it. You see how the skills and concepts you taught them have then been applied and developed. It's brilliant to see.

30 How to praise students

We know that students behave well in a climate that emphasises success and achievement, underpinned by clear expectations.

Being told that we are doing something well counts for a lot.

It means even more if we say it in person, so be careful not to be duped into the idea that the only way you can praise students is by using a formal system, such as stickers and comments in their planner.

Probably the most important sentence we can say to students is, 'I am really pleased with that', or suchlike.

So be ready to praise a lot and criticise a little.

That said, don't be drawn into issuing superficial and ultimately irrelevant praise. If a student has done something worthy of being told, 'well done', then say it, but don't get a reputation as someone who says 'awesome' or 'fantastic' for what is actually pretty mediocre.

If a student has done something that is worthwhile, say so. If it isn't, then say so.

Remember that, in most schools, there will be a repertoire of ways of saying well done, a panoply of systems for showing that a student has been successful. These might include:

- congratulating an individual publicly or privately;
- saying 'well done' to the whole class;

Teacher training

- writing a positive comment on a piece of work;
- writing a positive comment in the student's planner;
- issuing a 'well done' or commendation sticker;
- phoning the student's parents to say how pleased you are with progress;
- placing work on display or reading it out in a lesson;
- sending home a letter or postcard of congratulations;
- inviting the student to see a senior member of staff for personal praise;
- public praise in assemblies;
- the student's name being read aloud in an 'achievement assembly'.

Of all of these, possibly the most important is simply taking the student to one side, or catching him or her after the lesson, and saying, 'That piece of work you did – it was really impressive. Well done'.

The power of human interaction counts for a lot. Use it as much as you can.

TALKING POINTS

- Are there any missing items here – other ways of expressing praise that haven't been included?
- Which do you already use most?
- Which do you think you might start using more of?

31 How to be an effective tutor

When I am interviewing teachers for a post at school, I usually ask them how they feel about being a tutor.

The answers are usually the same: 'Oh, I love being a tutor – it's one of the best parts of the job'.

Sometimes, the response is more extreme: 'Oh, yes, headmaster, it would be a privilege to be a tutor'.

In reality, being a tutor is something that is expected of most teachers and yet is something we receive little training for and then have few opportunities to watch other tutors at work or to receive meaningful feedback on our work as a tutor.

As a result, the quality of tutoring in schools can be mixed – more mixed than the quality of teaching.

Being an effective tutor matters. There is plenty of evidence to show that the role of a tutor is an essential ingredient in the achievement, progress, attendance, personal development and social skills of a student.

The link between a young person and an interested, concerned adult who talks to them as an individual is at the core of our pastoral work.

The tutor is the person who has most consistent, day-to-day contact and is the essential link between the student, subject staff and home. The relationship between tutor and students is, therefore, an integral part of every teacher's role.

Here is how we can make a difference:

Contribute to students' personal and social development

- Show interest in students as individuals and enjoy working with them.
- Talk to them. According to Professor John West-Burnham, 60 per cent of students in secondary schools never have a conversation in school with an adult.
- Praise, encourage, motivate and chide them, as necessary.
- Learn about and celebrate their success, within and beyond school.
- Monitor the effects of changes at home and in school.
- Promote cooperative learning within the group.
- Create a group identity within which students feel secure and welcome.

Promote learning

- Promote interest in, and discussion about, how we learn.
- Provide advice on learning (e.g. revision and personal organisation).

Monitor and motivate

- Be vigilant about attendance and punctuality and insist that every student (irrespective of background) is properly dressed for school and has appropriate equipment for lessons.
- Maintain a daily register to record attendance and note lateness.

- Give a high profile to the need for good attendance and identify where absence levels may be falling into a pattern or causing concern.

- Know individuals' strengths and weaknesses.

- Monitor adherence to school expectations.

- Track students' progress, using various electronic or paper-based systems, and discuss their progress with them at key points in the school year.

- Liaise with parents and staff about student progress.

Provide support, welfare and guidance

- Help students through pivotal points in their education and career choices.

- Create a warm and supportive environment for personal and social development.

- Model appropriate behaviour, courtesy and respect.

The skill of being a tutor lies in creating routines that both enable you to address the whole group – reading out notices and so on – and give you space to interact with individuals and groups. As you gain confidence, you'll be able to build a small team of students within your tutor group who will take on responsibility for such tasks as making sure noticeboards are up-to-date.

You will also want to be able to create opportunities when students are, say, discussing a topic, when you will see some one to one or in small groups, to discuss their progress or their extra-curricular involvement.

These conversations reinforce your role as a tutor, cement the relationship you have with individual members of the group and help students to see how the school – via you – appreciates and takes interest in the activities they do beyond the classroom and, perhaps, beyond the school itself.

Teacher training

So don't underestimate the influence you might have as a tutor and, during your training or induction, try to get opportunities to watch different tutors at work. Watch how they manage routines, interact with students and set the tone for the day ahead.

TALKING POINTS

- What do you remember of tutor time from your own schooldays? Did it leave an impression? Positive or negative?
- Have you watched some tutors at work? What did the best of them do? What about the worst?

WHAT I LOVE ABOUT TEACHING

Whatever people say, teaching remains a very creative job. You have to think of ways of taking topics and issues and then make them relevant to young people of different interest levels and backgrounds.

32 How to assess whether you are any good as a tutor

It is all very well knowing what great tutors do. It is much more demanding to do it.

I recently asked a group of experienced heads of year to give me a list of the 'essential ingredients' in their most effective tutors. They came up with the list of ingredients below, which I have converted into a self-evaluation sheet.

If we really think being a tutor is so important (and I do), then we ought to be constantly monitoring how well we are doing.

Our most effective tutors:

- know and care about students in their tutor groups;
- see monitoring and target-setting as a core part of their job;
- understand the need to work with students on skills beyond the classroom – emotions, motivation, social skills, courtesy, how to speak appropriately in difficult circumstances;
- are well organised and manage time well;
- listen actively;
- pay attention to small details – courtesy, words of thanks;
- treat poor behaviour as simply a choice and good behaviour as a characteristic;
- apologise when they do something wrong or inappropriate;

- catch students being good far more than they catch them getting it wrong – in other words, they give a lot of genuine praise to students and use the school's systems to record students' wider achievements;
- take an interest in students' lives and experiences, while maintaining professional boundaries.

These provide a helpful, aspirational starting point as you set out on being a really successful tutor.

One problem (though it might not feel like a problem) is that you don't get formally observed as a tutor very often and, therefore, get little feedback from colleagues on how you are doing.

You could decide to review your tutoring each term or so, supplementing your self-evaluation with some anonymous comments from your tutor group. A simple questionnaire to students such as the following, used, say, twice a year, might help you to see whether the purpose of tutor time sometimes needs to be articulated more clearly.

1   Do you enjoy tutor time?

2   Does it help you in your other lessons or in achieving well in school generally?

3   How could we improve tutor time?

Questionnaires such as this don't have to feel in any way undermining to you in your role, especially if you are presenting them to the tutor group in the spirit of, 'So what do we need to do to keep improving tutor time? Give me your feedback, and we'll work on it as a group after the half-term break'.

In other words, you are working with students as part of a collective project – hence asking them for their feedback.

Then there's self-evaluation. A simple checklist such as in Table 32.1 is used in some schools to help tutors reflect on the aspects of their role. If we know what bits of tutoring seem to count, then why not focus on doing them as well as possible? That is the rationale for the self-assessment checklist.

Table 32.1 Self-assessment checklist

Climate for learning	*Never*	*Sometimes*	*Mostly*	*Always*
My tutor base has a tutor group noticeboard				
The noticeboard is up-to-date with notices and announcements				
The noticeboard is maintained by one or two students				
The noticeboard contains some distinctive material, e.g. tally of commendation totals, photographs of students in the group etc.				
I ensure that students are only dismissed once the room has been left tidy				

Expectations				
Students in my tutor group know that they must be properly dressed				
Students are silent for the register and take it seriously				
Students listen when others are speaking and give positive feedback to one another				
Students are in a routine of having their planner signed and know that I will make an issue of it if it is not				
I keep my register accurately, note down reasons for lateness and forward absence letters to the attendance officer immediately				
I try to create a sense of order				

Table 32.1 *continued*

Climate for learning	*Never*	*Sometimes*	*Mostly*	*Always*

Leadership and involvement

I give students some defined
roles, e.g. register or notices
collection, noticeboard monitors,
'Thought for the week' announcer

I talk to students about their
involvement in out-of-hours learning

Relationships

I talk to students during tutor time,
either as a class or in small groups

On duty, I talk to students

I contact parents (after talking to
pastoral head) where there is a
concern about a student in my
tutor group

Impact on learning

Students in my tutor group know
their target grades across subjects

I am able to talk about students'
strengths and weaknesses

I use some tutor time to talk about
planning, note-making, participation,
behaviour, listening skills, revision
techniques, standards

TALKING POINTS

- What is your view of the role of a tutor?
- What skills do you think you can bring to the role?
- What do you need to develop?

Part IV

Becoming a teacher

So here you are: on the verge, or maybe in the early stages, of becoming a teacher. Welcome to a noble and essential profession.

Veterans are likely to tell you that your true training begins now. They will imply that you only get a genuine grip on the realities of teaching by doing the job day in and day out.

There is some truth in that, but a balanced training will have provided you with a combination of philosophical principles ('why teaching matters') and techniques ('how to introduce Boyle's Law').

This is when the job can start to become daunting. The start of a new school year is always characterised by sunny optimism. However nervous you feel, there is an energy, a freshness, that will carry you from your induction day, through the summer holidays, through the initial training day and into your first encounter with classes.

It will be a roller-coaster, of course, but you will feel supported and energised and – mostly – happy. Your training will have helped you.

However, the darker days of early autumn then arrive. People – such as colleagues and students – forget that you are a fledgling teacher. Their attention is on themselves. You feel more isolated, more unnoticed, more vulnerable. This is where a sense of moral purpose, combined with serious coping strategies, matter a lot.

Your career is about to get started. First, let's get that job.

33 | How to apply for a teaching job

Your training is well under way, and you are sure that teaching as a career is for you. Now, it is time to secure a job as a teacher. This chapter takes you through some key elements.

Choose wisely

I will leave out the obvious stuff about deciding where, geographically, you want to work and what the different considerations might be about teaching in an inner-city or rural school. If you are turning into an effective teacher, you are more than capable of doing the groundwork on areas and types of school, without advice from me.

My only comment on the type of school is to take a long-term view. It is much rarer for a teacher to move from the independent sector into a state school, for example. Partly, this may be because, once teachers settle into working in an independent school, they are more likely to stay. It may be that, having found a niche in a school they like, teachers are less inclined to apply to move into a sector they are less familiar with or even slightly wary of. It may even be the case that state school heads, on receiving an application from someone whose experience is in a small, independent school, assume that the applicant's experience and knowledge of curriculum and other developments are not best suited to their type of school.

All of these are, of course, assumptions, and each may contain an element of stereotyping or misinformation, but that is my point: if you are a teacher with aspirations of career progression, you might wish to reflect on whether the school you apply for at the very start of your career is likely to close off any opportunities for movement between schools, or promotion within the school, in the future.

We will return to 'getting promoted' nearer the end of the book.

Apply carefully

You will research the schools you wish to apply for using various websites (e.g. TES) and other sources (e.g. word of mouth), and so, again, I will not cover the obvious stuff about looking at the school's website, reading its Ofsted reports and suchlike.

Instead, note that, from the moment you submit an application, you are being judged. If you apply for a job at my school, and your application has a typing error in the first line, then I am likely to reject it on the grounds that your standards aren't high enough. Similarly, if you can't distinguish between 'its' (the pronoun, like 'her/his/their', as in, 'this is a school where its beliefs and values are clear') and 'it's' (a contraction of 'it is', as in, 'it's a school I would love to work at'), then either expect not to get called to interview, or expect that, if you do make it to interview, I will be asking you to explain to me the difference between the two words and then asking why you didn't get it right in your letter.

This isn't because I am a heartless and loathsome monster who likes to humiliate rookie interview candidates. It is actually rather more about values. I believe that, if we are to appoint someone to teach young people, and in the process pay them a not inconsiderable salary, then we should expect that some very basic elements have been got right. Appearances matter, and accuracy matters. You need to show that from the outset, with an application that is accurate, well laid out, clear and concise.

None of that is as easy, nor perhaps as difficult, as it seems.

Make time to apply properly

This will seem like common sense, but that won't stop me from saying it. Most of us feel we don't have sufficient time, amid the giddying frenzy of modern life. We always seem to be on the proverbial back foot, desperately trying to catch up with the madcap list of tasks we have set ourselves to achieve.

It can seem that we are always reacting to the agendas set by others, rather than doing what we want, or need, to do.

Thus something as important as applying for a job can be squeezed to the margins of our daily life. It can end up being done in the early hours, in a hurry, in a time and space where we can't quite find enough time to give it our full attention.

That can lead us to write too quickly and to make mistakes – whether of a typographical nature or by not fully matching our application to the stated requirements of the school.

Getting a post in a school you want to work at is important. It will shape the trajectory of your future career as a teacher. So push some of the distracting other stuff to the sidelines for most of an evening or two and concentrate on creating an application that achieves what you need it to achieve: getting you an interview.

> ### TALKING POINTS
>
> - Think back to before you began your training? What were your expectations of being a teacher? How have they changed?
> - What are the main messages from your training so far?
> - What single word sums up your attitude to becoming a fully fledged teacher?

34 How to write a good letter of application

There is a separate chapter in this book on what good writing looks like. It is designed to help you to write clear, concise, informative reports and memos.

This chapter, however, is instead all about how to write an effective job application.

Remember that you don't write a letter of application to get you the job; you write it to get you an interview. It therefore needs to be easy to read and interesting.

Here are my five suggestions for writing an effective letter of application:

1 Keep it concise – two sides of A4 maximum. Use short paragraphs, making the letter easier to read. Where they bring clarity, use subheadings to divide your letter into different topics and use bullet-points where it is useful to list some specific examples.

2 Address the letter to the headteacher/principal unless told otherwise.

3 If you really want this job, then match your letter precisely to what the school is saying it is looking for. If it sends a 'person specification' with a two-column list of its 'essential' and 'preferable' lists of skills, qualities and experiences, then see if,

in your letter, you can refer explicitly to as many of those items as possible. And if, like me, you like to make things explicit for the reader, put each of them in bold text, so that they jump off the page a little.

4   Write about your specific experience, rather than your generalised educational philosophy. So don't write:

> I believe that every student is an individual and the role of a good teacher is to address his or her learning needs. The best teachers individualise their teaching to the differentiated requirements of every young person in the class, thereby making the topic relevant to each one, whether she is gifted and talented or has special educational needs in literacy.

To my mind, this is just a platitude. It is the kind of thing we hear all the time. You want your letter to give much more of a sense of who you are and what you believe and to exemplify this through what you actually have done. For example:

> I believe that every student should be treated as an individual. In my teaching so far I have demonstrated this in several ways: first, I have planned my lessons knowing that different students will need different levels of guidance and support. This has helped me to tailor my teaching to their learning.
>
> Second, I have always made time to talk to students who are struggling, or who are showing exceptional promise. I have wanted them to know that I have noticed and can help them further.
>
> Finally, I have taken part in extra-curricular activities at lunchtime (including helping to coach the school netball team) and after school (intervention classes for struggling students). These enrichments have allowed me to demonstrate that I can work with students in different contexts and treat them as individuals.

5   Proofread your letter and application form very carefully. Don't make the mistake of leaving in the name of a headteacher of a different school, where you have done a quick search and replace from an existing letter. Get someone else to check it through for you too. First impressions matter. If you are going to the effort of submitting a job application, make it impressive, attractive and accurate.

TALKING POINTS

- Any surprises here?
- Who might you ask to read through a first draft of your letter to give you constructive feedback?

WHAT I LOVE ABOUT TEACHING

The laughs - with colleagues and with students. Being an adult is sometimes to be surrounded by people moaning. Often with young people there's loads of optimism and lots of laughter. It can raise your spirits.

How different application letters compare

Reading advice is often useful. However – as in the classroom – sometimes it is useful to have some models to help us to see what other applicants have included or omitted from their letters, so that you can reflect on what you would or would not do in yours.

These examples are real letters of application for a post. Some details have been changed.

My suggestion, for each letter, is that you read it looking at what you (a) like and (b) dislike in terms of both content and style. Make some notes for yourself, and I will provide a brief commentary at the end.

LETTER 1

After completing my teacher training in 2010 I took the decision to commence my teaching career in Derbyshire. During this time I believe I established myself as an effective and proactive teacher and relished meeting the challenges of my new career. Having grown up in Norfolk I have taken the decision to return to the area to continue developing in this role.

I am now covering maternity leave in Derby and this is due to end at Christmas or shortly thereafter. The experience of my first two years of teaching has provided me with the knowledge and confidence to do this.

Becoming a teacher

In my previous post I undertook several responsibilities in the absence of a head of department. This included being accredited as Lead Internal Verifier for the BTEC Music courses levels two and three, both of which were introduced just over two years ago. In order to gain this status I had to undergo an online assessment and submit samples of work to Edexcel in order for them to monitor our practice. This process involved analysing data, assessing the marking of teachers from other BTEC centres and that of teachers within the department, and submitting a report to Edexcel on our progress in developing best practice for both courses. I was able to highlight existing good practice and points for improvement, and following the report from Edexcel in response to this I rewrote schemes of work for several units and created new resources in order to improve the delivery of the course across the department. This also required the adaptation of methods of evidence collection and the cultivation of new assessment styles in order to meet the criteria of the specification precisely, and through collaborative working with BTEC department leaders I was able to trial and implement some of these changes. This process consolidated my ability to lead the development of a course based on a detailed specification and take responsibility for the level of success achieved by our learners.

Extra-curricular activities are extremely important to the overall development and progress of all students and I am passionate about involving as many pupils and members of staff as possible in a range of musical activities. Throughout my teaching career I have led and supported a range of ensembles including choirs, chamber groups and orchestras. In my two years at Stanton High School I ran a West African Drumming ensemble that performed at several events in and out of school, including an African themed wedding. I also led the organisation of larger extra-curricular events such as a 'Battle of the Bands' competition earlier this year. I am currently running a keyboard club aiming to develop the theory skills of students at key stage three and providing vocal support and piano accompaniment during show rehearsals.

For the past two years I have been teaching AS and A level music technology. During my years as a freelance musician I gathered a wealth of skills and experiences and became adaptable to a range of professional situations. As a teacher I believe that drawing on these years helps me enormously to bring a similar range of experiences to students both in and out of the classroom. I always aim to expose learners to new musical styles and ideas that they may not have had access to before. This includes looking at music from around the world in real contexts, the role of real musicians in society and keeping up with contemporary artists and changes in the music industry.

I am a friendly, approachable person who enjoys building strong working relationships with colleagues and students, and I believe that these are the foundation of successful learning and progression. I am good humoured and calm in the face of stressful situations and strive to be a 'real' person at all times. I became a teacher to inspire the enjoyment and appreciation of music in young people by providing them with the opportunities that I have been lucky enough to be presented with in my life, and I would relish the opportunity to continue doing this in Suffolk schools.

LETTER 2

I am confident that I would be an excellent candidate for this position. I have wanted to teach English at your school since I was inspired by my experience of the subject as a student at the school myself. Although my training in Leeds has been truly valuable and enjoyable, I have always hoped to settle in my home town and, ideally, invest back in the community and very school that opened so many doors for me.

I know you are a really good school, striving for outstanding teaching and learning across the curriculum. I am proud of the fact that at this early stage in my career, I am delivering consistently good lessons in particularly challenging circumstances.

I am deeply passionate about the subject I teach and my thirst for learning means my excellent subject knowledge is ever growing. Thus far, I have taught a wide range of topics and age ranges across the subject. These include: Contemporary Drama, Shakespeare, Letter and CV Writing, Teen-fiction, Media and Non-fiction, Roald Dahl, Dickens, Gothic Horror, Animation, Film

Reviews, Poetry (Contemporary and Heritage), The Modern Novel, Creative Writing and Spoken Language.

I understand that good behaviour management skills are vital for outstanding teaching and learning. In the particularly challenging school in which I currently work, I enjoy the challenge of finding creative and innovative ways to inspire and engage our students and in turn find it deeply rewarding. I hope you would agree that a consistent, 'firm but fair' approach to the school's behaviour management policy is central to effective behaviour management. I believe that an approachable teacher is important to the students, as is one who can acknowledge the positives and brings out the best in students. I am proud of the fact that I have an excellent relationship with all my students and know that I played a crucial part in helping them fulfil their potential.

Finally, I know that a good school requires brilliant staff and in addition to the classroom-based responsibility, a teacher's role involves team-work and the sharing of good practice, efficiency and meticulous attention to detail, maintaining accurate records, writing reports and suchlike. I will do all of these things to the best of my ability.

LETTER 3

I feel incredibly lucky to have had the opportunity to change my career direction into an area which excites and motivates me. My lifelong fascination of Geography and the constant desire to share and impart my knowledge of the subject, led me to commence a Geography PGCE course. Throughout the course I have developed both personally and academically and have thrived on all the challenges presented to me.

Teaching is where I am meant to be and my goal is to share my passion so students develop a lifelong interest and a sense of awe and wonder of the world around them. Observational placements at various schools have presented different challenges, all of which have enhanced my teaching toolkit. However one factor remains consistent, if students are provided with a safe, supportive, stimulating learning environment they will develop and it is this ethos that draws me to your school.

I note from your website the large amount of extra-curricular activities, which particularly impress me and I firmly agree that success in the classroom is also supported and complimented by success and participation in extra activities of a student's choice. It is a school with such beliefs and ethos that I wish to be a part of as I develop into the role as a teacher.

I firmly believe that the classroom must provide the appropriate atmosphere for learning and this is an area which I try to maintain when planning and implementing lessons. Students should not fear expressing themselves and should look forward to lessons in an environment that is not only supporting and stimulating, but also one that challenges the mind. I believe students should be encouraged to raise questions and my motto for teaching is 'the only stupid question is the one you do not ask!'

I therefore effectively plan stimulating classes with good assessment opportunities ensuring that students are motivated and encouraged in believing they can achieve goals and raise attainment standards. Within the classroom, I endeavour to provide lesson plans that cater for all learning styles, with the use of power point, film clips and promote hands on activities for visual, auditory and kinaesthetic learners.

I am conscious of the need to adapt the learning environment to support a student, teach them as an individual, while ensuring that they experience high quality learning. I strive to achieve this through reflective practice, the ability to listen and also to act upon advice of colleagues in order to develop my teaching to the highest standard.

In order to integrate within the team and school life at my current school, I have volunteered to help out with the Year 9 rugby team. An extracurricular activity which is not only rewarding but I believe essential, if pupil respect is to be obtained and relationships built. From experience I recognise that pupils need to see that teachers are also 'doers' and not just people who they see as classroom based. Such exercises, demonstrate that teachers are human too,

> and I believe, assist in forming a firm teacher/student relationship which should be carried over into the classroom.
>
> Involvement in extra-curricular activities is something I am keen to support.

So, what do you think? Which letter grabs your interest the most and why? Which do you find least successful?

My comments

A letter of application has a single purpose: to get you invited to interview. At that point, you will be able to demonstrate your skills and qualities in person. Don't, therefore, view the letter as needing to cover everything. Never write more than two sides of A4. Never use a font size smaller than 12 point. Keep paragraphs short and clear. Use subheadings or bullet points if they add clarity.

In a letter I would look for:

- some passion about teaching;
- some passion about the subject;
- an outline of the experience/skills you would bring to our school.

Letter 1

A good letter, it outlines a promising range of experience. It is mostly accessible, though it gets bogged down in the middle with (to my mind) excess detail. It combines passion with detail. It would be clearer with subheadings and shorter paragraphs, but that may just be my personal preference.

Letter 2

This is a bit general at times. It talks about a passion for the subject, but I would want to see more specific examples. It uses too many points about what the candidate 'would do' if appointed, rather than providing directly relevant evidence of experience.

Letter 3

This one is quirkier. You get a real sense of the voice of the writer. It would benefit from some specific examples of topics and activities that have been taught, and a bit more reflection on the impact of these. It is strong on extra-curricular engagement.

My own order of preference for these letters is 1, 3, 2.

TALKING POINTS

So, consider these three letters of application. Imagine that they were all applying for the same post at a school run by you:

- What would your rank order be, and why?
- Which applicants would you call to interview?
- Take the best letter: how might it be improved?

---

36 How to be successful at interview

If you have got the letter right, then you will get an interview. This section gives you advice on how to approach what will undoubtedly be a stressful day, and to help you to be both successful in gaining the job (if you want it) and in making sure that you learn from the experience for future reference.

Invitation to interview

The turnaround time in schools from applications being received to candidates being invited to interview is generally much quicker than it used to be. That is partly because the race to recruit the best candidates has got fiercer, and partly because communication makes it quicker. No longer, in general, do we spend a few days reflecting on a final shortlist of candidates and then writing and posting out individual invitations.

Instead, especially towards the ends of appointment periods (October half-term, February half-term and, especially, May half-term), if a promising application arrives by email, we may well phone the applicant straight away and invite them to interview. It will depend on the number of applications and the urgency of securing a teacher for the available post.

Most schools will contact you initially by telephone, with a personnel administrator or the headteacher's personal assistant leaving a message if necessary. This will be saying that the school has received your application and wants to invite you to interview.

If you can, write down what is said to you, because chances are you will be asked to teach a lesson during the interview day. It is easy, in the giddiness of receiving an out-of-the-blue phone call like this not really to hear the detail of what is said. So write it down.

Ideally, you will need to know:

- for the day:

    –what time to arrive and where (e.g. reception);

- for the lesson:

    –what topic (if any) they want you to teach;

    –which year/ability the group might be;

    –how many will be in the class;

    –how long the lesson is expected to last;

    –what resources (e.g. interactive whiteboard/wifi) will be available;

    –who will be observing.

Chances are you won't get the chance to ask all of this, and so it is important to ask whether an email message confirming the arrangements is going to be sent, and whether it is possible to send any queries once you have received it.

Then, enthusiastically, say you would be delighted to accept and look forward to coming to the school on the given date.

Preparing for interview

Once you have the date of the interview and the details of what will be expected of you, there will be some practical issues of preparation. Most important of these is the thought that goes into planning for an observed lesson. This is something that you will inevitably worry about. Everybody does. It is an artificial task and needs to be seen in that light. I have devoted the next chapter to giving some specific advice, but the main message is: keep it simple. You may be tempted to put together a pedagogical cabaret that involves using card sorts, washing lines, varieties of groupings, no-hands-up, and all kinds of other techniques that you might, with your own classes, deploy from time to time.

Save those for when you have got the job. For this dummy lesson, plan something simple that doesn't rely on technology or last-minute photocopying of too many resources in the school you are visiting.

You owe it to yourself to keep your stress levels under control.

It might be that you have a number of questions about either the lesson or the arrangements for the day. If so, email whoever sent you the confirmation of the invitation to interview – for example the headteacher's personal assistant. But send just one email containing your queries, not a barrage of separate emails. He or she is likely to receive 100 or more messages a day, and one thing you definitely don't want to do is to be perceived, on the day of the interview, as 'the one who kept pestering me with questions'.

You will also need to look at the practicalities of travelling to the interview. If it is a long way, then you will need to stay locally the night before. All of these issues – including, perhaps, the need to ask the school to book you accommodation for the night before the interview – you won't need advice from me on.

All I would say is manage your stress by building in lots of margin-of-error time. When candidates arrive flustered for an interview because they have been stuck in traffic, or have endured one of those bizarre train delays where, for no reason, the train has come to an unexpected standstill in the middle of nondescript countryside, they are wrong-footed from the outset, and it takes them a while to settle back into the rhythm of an already highly charged day.

If that means that you arrive at the school an hour early, find somewhere (such as in your car) where you can sit and observe staff and students arriving. This will give you a flavour of the place where you may, in fewer than eight hours, find that you will end up working. Watch especially students' conduct as they arrive. Does it represent the school well? Are there signs, in the run-up to the formal start of the day, of staff being on duty to welcome students and thereby send out the message that the school's values prevail as soon as someone steps through the school gates? Do you get a feeling of calm purpose?

Then, head to reception earlier than the designated time, but not too much earlier. Schools take time each day to get cranked up into their ritualistic rhythms. If you arrive before most of the staff, and especially the receptionist, then you will simply be an irritant. If the start of the interview day is 9:00, get to reception around 8:45. Then, you can aim to sign in, relax a little and begin to see who you're up against for the job.

Interview dress code

Dress to impress. It is as simple as that. If you turn up at a school like ours – a large, state comprehensive – and you aren't dressed formally and smartly, then I am going to wonder whether this reflects a casualness of attitude. Wear a suit, or at least a jacket and tie, or the female equivalent of that kind of formality. Have clean shoes.

Your dress code should not be 'smart casual'; it should be smart.

Interacting throughout the day

On an interview day, you are being interviewed all the time. Possibly only when you use the toilet are you not being judged. So don't be lured into thinking that some parts of the day simply don't matter. If students are being asked to show you around the school, they may well be asked which candidate they would prefer. That doesn't mean they are doing any more than giving an opinion. But it does have implications for you: you don't want to be seen as 'the one who talked all the time' (there usually is someone like that at interview), or 'the one who didn't seem interested'.

Becoming a teacher

So my advice for conducting yourself through the interview day is as follows:

- Be cautious: you are on display. Play it cool. Don't talk too much. Don't look too serious. Don't be openly critical of any aspect of the school to anyone.

- Be reflective: use the day to learn as much as you can – about the school and about yourself. This means wandering, talking to people, having conversations with students, cleaners, caretakers, the receptionist.

- Be canny: throughout the day, think about what you like about the school and what you think could be improved. As an ice-breaker at the start of interviews, I sometimes ask: 'What are your impressions of our school?' or 'What have you seen in our school that you like?' This is often a cue for obsequiousness. Then I will fire off the killer rejoinder: 'And what could we improve?' Here, in truth, you want an answer that is true but relatively inoffensive. The reason: if you say something along the lines of, 'behaviour is pretty bad' or 'staff morale seems terrible', then, except with the most robust, self-flagellating of headteachers, you are probably committing a kamikaze act of recklessness.

- Headteachers won't want to hear some devastating critique of their school's ethos or some hint that there is a deep-riven problem at the core of the school. Choose instead an area of the school that looks dowdy and would benefit from some visual pizzazz; or choose an aspect of the school that isn't yet fully developed and show how you could supplement it – 'you don't seem to have a debating society, if I understand correctly: it's the kind of extra-curricular project I would really like to run'.

TALKING POINT

- What are the main lessons for you from this advice?

---

37 How to teach a lesson at interview

When I interview prospective teachers, I always try to put the lesson into context by saying something like this:

> You are being asked to teach a lesson as part of the interview process today. My guess is that it's the part of the day that you're least looking forward to. But we know it's artificial and will be amazed if you teach your all-time-best lesson. You won't know the students, or their names, or precisely what level they are working at. So of course it's artificial. And you may end up teaching a not-very good lesson.
>
> But understand that the purpose is to help us imagine whether we can see you in our school, teaching our students. It helps us to get a feel for what you may be like in our context. And, if you get through to the interview this afternoon, we will ask you how you feel the lesson went, and how you might have taught it differently. If it was a bad lesson, we won't worry too much unless, if we ask that question, you say you think it was brilliant!
>
> In other words, asking you to teach a lesson, however artificial, and then talking to you about it helps us to see whether what we have here is someone who is reflective, keen to improve, and genuinely interested in the process of teaching.

Becoming a teacher

In reality, this probably reassures anxious candidates not a bit. But it's important that I say it, and we genuinely mean it: the lesson is a springboard to a conversation later in the interview process.

For this reason, I would advise that your 'interview lesson' is not planned as a complex circus act designed to entertain whoever observes you. Keep it simple. Partly, this is so that you aren't fretting about issues that are beyond your control – such as what kind of interactive whiteboard they have and whether you will be able to make it work. Partly, it is because people make judgements very quickly about the quality of what they see: the more you can be yourself, confident, undistracted and focused on the essential elements of what you want students to learn, the more you are likely to impress.

At most schools, you won't be teaching a full lesson in any case. At our school, it is likely to be just thirty minutes, which is all the more reason to stick to a simple, uncluttered format.

Keeping it simple, for me, involves using a clear, straightforward structure and minimising aspects that could go wrong. That is because I am a control freak and don't want to add to the stresses that will inevitably be there on the day of the interview.

A simple lesson structure might be as shown in Table 37.1.

It shows a simple, 'bread and butter' lesson structure. It does not aim to be some flashy classroom cabaret, designed to prompt the applause of your dutiful observers.

Instead, it is designed to show that you can teach and that, when you do, students learn things.

You will, of course, want to make your own decision about how you approach the challenge of an observed lesson, with students you don't know, in a classroom you don't know, in a school you (probably) don't know well.

My advice: keep it simple.

TALKING POINTS

- What are the main messages for you in all of this?
- Is there anything that you instinctively disagree with?

Table 37.1 Simple lesson structure

Lesson element	Purpose
1 An introduction to who you are; asking students to make name cards; introduction to the topic and what you expect students to learn in the next 30 minutes or so	Establish your authority; make it easier to engage with students because you will be able to use their names; suggest you are well organised; use routines to calm your nerves
2 An initial activity in which students are exploring the topic (a clear, straightforward handout that gets them puzzling something out, problem-solving, making predictions, working in pairs or threes)	Show that you can structure activities to build development of a skill or knowledge. In the interview, be ready to talk about how you would group students for the activity, that is, be ready to talk about differentiating the task for different groups
3 Some feedback from students in which they demonstrate what they have just learned, or what problems they may have encountered and then solved	Demonstrate your classroom management, your ability to run a discussion, your handling of Q&A activities
4 Some more extended activity, perhaps with students writing something to summarise/demonstrate what they have learned. Then they compare each other's work, giving feedback using criteria or a framework that you have provided	Show that you can move students into deeper, more independent learning, and that you know the importance of providing an assessment framework/modelling the kind of language they should use
5 Wrap up: you might ask students a big question ('so using your own words, explain to me why . . ./how . . .') or ask them to think of one or two things they now know or can do that they couldn't at the start of the lesson. Thank them for making you so welcome. Then collect any handouts/name badges, thank the group again, say goodbye and leave	Show that, even in a short time with a class you don't know, you can demonstrate that they have learned things. It is calm, efficient, reassuring, clear and purposeful, and has the advantage for you that it is not reliant on technology

38 How to manage parents' evenings

Schools organise parents' evenings in a variety of ways. Some call them other things. They may be 'consultation evenings' or 'target-setting days', but at their heart is the idea that parents should meet a teacher who is responsible for their child's progress.

You may be there as subject teacher or, as is more frequent in many schools, as tutor or 'learning mentor' with responsibility to report on progress across the student's various subjects.

Whatever the format of the meetings, they are important, and a few tips may help you to be more confident about approaching your first few and making sure the parents you meet find them productive.

Know your students

Sometimes, especially early on in the year, it can be difficult, out of context, to put the right face to a student's name, so have your class or tutor group list in front of you, with a printout of the photographs that most schools will have on their management systems. This will help you to feel confident that you are talking to the right parent about the right child.

Know your students' data

Too often, parents' evenings can have a blandness to them. They can be too unspecific. Their essential message from each teacher can be little more than, 'If she works harder then she will do better'.

Parents should, rightly, expect more than this. So the skill of the teacher is in being able to give a concise, clear account of what the child is doing well in and then suggesting one or two very specific aspects of the subject that the student should do more of or less of in order to improve.

For a Year 10 student in English, this might go something like this:

> Emily is working well in English. She has done all the reading I've asked her to do, and tells me that she has enjoyed the texts. Her writing about literature is getting more precise, and she has suddenly understood that using short quotations embedded into her own sentences makes writing much more specific. She's got a target for the end of the course of a B, but could exceed that if she looks at making her writing more interesting. That involves pausing and thinking of more specific, vivid vocabulary, and trying to use a range of shorter and longer sentences. Being interesting as a writer is one of the big differences between a B and an A or A* grade, so working on her writing will be essential. You could support her by encouraging her to keep reading, and perhaps having times at home or on holiday which are specifically for reading, not being online or playing computer games.

On the page that will feel artificial, and it certainly won't match everyone's style. That is not my point. We want teachers to be distinctive and individual, not robotic. However, we also want to make sure that if, after a conversation with their child's teacher, we said to the parent, 'So what's going well, and what could be improved?', they could give an answer beyond a bland platitude.

Manage the meeting

Nothing infuriates parents more than poor time-keeping at consultation evenings. It is not uncommon to see queues at some teachers' desks that resemble the Soviet citizenry of the 1970s waiting their turn to buy bread.

If you have five-minute appointment slots for each parent, then work on the assumption that you have four minutes. Have a very clear formula and stick to it.

My suggestion would involve a routine such as this:

- Call the name of the next parent on your list. This is important. Don't just take the next parent who turns up: stick rigidly to the allotted order. Do this by calling out the name of the student: 'Emily Edmonds'.

- Stand up and shake the hand of the parents or carers.

- Ask them if there is anything they want to ask/comment on about their child's progress in your subject. This is useful, as it gets any 'issues' into the open immediately. In most cases, parents will say 'No, we'd just like to hear how she's doing'.

- Outline the strengths, giving specific examples of how the student has shown progress.

- Outline one or two key areas for development. Say something like, 'Does that all make sense? Is it clear?' The parents will, most likely, say 'Yes'.

- Stand up, saying thank you and shaking their hand. Call out the next child's name.

If that sounds mechanical or soulless, it is not: it is a routine that is well-managed, helpful to parents, informative and professional. Use an approach like this, and parents will appreciate it, and you will develop a reputation for being both efficient and proficient.

TALKING POINTS

- What are your own memories of parents' evenings – or are you from the era when students never attended them?
- What do you think they are designed to achieve?
- Have you had a chance to observe a parents' evening?
- What did you learn from it?

WHAT I DISLIKE ABOUT TEACHING

At some points in the year you get bogged down in writing reports. In my subject (RE) I teach lots of students just once a week. It means I have far more reports than most people, and yet no one really takes account of this.

39 How to deal with parental complaints at parents' evenings

Sometimes, parents are in a mood to complain. Don't take it too personally. If you have children, you may be similarly frustrated one day. The key to all these tales of adversity is to retain some perspective.

If a parent is fuming, it will usually be based on one of two scenarios:

- You or the school has made a mistake.
- They believe that you or the school has made a mistake, but actually you haven't: they have got the wrong information, probably from their child.

Here is how the parents' consultation may play out. You call out the name of the next student on your list. Two parents come forward. You do your 'hello' routine. They respond frostily, and you sense that something is going to go wrong.

This is the point at which to hold your nerve and ask them if there is anything they would like to ask about, discuss or draw to your attention at the outset. Then stay quiet and listen.

The kinds of complaint you might get could include:

- We were told our child would be in a higher set and she isn't. We have complained to the head of year/head of department and had no response. We're not happy about it.

- Our son says that he can't concentrate in lessons because a small group of students keep messing about, and you don't seem to do anything about it.

- The school's homework policy says that our daughter should get some homework every week. She hasn't had any homework in your subject for three weeks. Why not?

- We emailed you two days ago asking what we should be doing at home to support our son's work. We haven't heard back from you yet. Why not?

- We've been looking through our daughter's book and notice that she has made a number of errors, including spellings, which you haven't corrected. How is she supposed to get better in the subject if you aren't giving her feedback?

Whether you are a new teacher or a gnarled veteran like me, questions such as this can seem confrontational and designed to undermine you. You should do all you can not to allow yourself to be antagonised by them. Schools traditionally haven't always been good at dealing with complaints at the earliest opportunity, and this leads some parents to become more vociferous than they need to be.

Stage 1: acknowledge the issue

With the complaints above, some are in your control; others may not be. For example, the complaint about setting may be something that is decided by the head of department and is beyond your area of influence. A response to an issue such as that is not to palm it off on to someone else and leave the parents thinking it is not being dealt with. Better to acknowledge the parents' frustration and say that you will do something to try to resolve the situation.

Note that saying something like 'I'm sorry you are feeling that your concern hasn't been addressed' will often prove very helpful for parents. They will hear an acknowledgement of an existing issue, rather than feeling they are being fobbed off with excuses or denials.

In reality, you are not apologising for an error: you are apologising that the parents feel there has been an error. It is an important, if subtle, distinction, because you are not actually conceding that their complaint is warranted; rather, you are expressing sympathy for the way they are feeling.

Stage 2: propose a course of action

Having acknowledged that the parents feel that there is an issue that has not been addressed, propose what will happen next. With the setting issue (the first complaint), you might say:

> Decisions about setting are made by the head of department in consultation with a student's teachers. I'm not sure what decision has been made about your daughter's group, but I will talk to Mr Houlton tomorrow and try to ensure that you have received a response – either by telephone or email – by the end of the day. That way, at least you will know where the decision-making is up to and be able to follow it up, if necessary, with Mr Houlton in person. Is that all right? There's probably nothing else I can do for now except to give you some feedback on how Laura is getting on in my lessons and what she needs to do if she's to make even more progress.

This response gives a pretty clear-cut commitment to the parents that they will receive a response within twenty-four hours. To my mind, this is courteous practice. However, if you say it, you'll need to ensure that it happens – otherwise the parent is going to become more irate.

Stage 3: do something

Having said you would ask the head of department to get back to the parents, I would suggest you send an email that night (yes –

get it out of the way, so that there is no unfinished business next day) to the head of department, saying something like:

Dear Paul

Mr and Mrs Reeves were concerned at the parents' evening tonight that they hadn't heard anything about the set Laura should be in. I said that it was something you were working on and that you would get back to them by email or phone by the end of tomorrow. Hope that's okay.

Then, when you next see the head of department, say, 'Not sure whether you've seen it yet but I sent an email about Laura Reeves and setting following last night's parents' evening. I said you'd get back to them about it'.

All of this represents a polite, purposeful and professional way of dealing with a parent's concern.

TALKING POINTS

- Have you had to deal with issues like these?
- What did you do?
- Which part of this advice feels especially helpful or unworkable to you?

40 How to deal with a personal complaint against you

Sometimes, parents' evenings turn nasty. It is not often, but they can do. Parents arrive with an irritation, a complaint, a vendetta – and you are in the line of fire.

If the complaint is about you, as some of the issues in the previous chapter may be, then your response will depend upon whether you think it is justified or not.

This is where openness trumps defensiveness.

If you haven't marked books for three weeks, or there are some students who are causing difficulties in your class, you are better giving an explanation rather than making excuses. You might say something like:

> You're absolutely right that our general policy is to mark students' books. I'm afraid that over the past fortnight we have had Year 11 mock exams and it has meant that I've had to concentrate on those. I meant to ask students to write a note in their homework diaries that their homework for the past two weeks was revision and research, but I forgot. My apologies. You'll notice that we're back on track next week.

The behaviour issue is trickier, because none of us likes to be accused of having poor classroom management. However, if there is a core of truth in the complaint, it might be best to respond like this:

When I took on the group in September I was told that there were a handful of students who had a bit of a reputation. They'd been something of a problem last year. So I have deliberately sat them in places where they are separate and worked with their head of year if their behaviour has been unacceptable or if they haven't completed their homework. So I'm disappointed that Laura thinks they are still problematic because I thought we had been making good progress to get them to behave much better. I'll use your comment – anonymously of course – to say to them and to pass on to their parents that other students and their parents are now complaining about the effect their conduct is having on their learning, and that this will raise the stakes. Thanks for bringing the issue to my attention and rest assured that we are dealing with these students.

Now, this might do the trick, satisfying the parents' concern, or it might not. Certainly use the complaint to make something of an issue with the students who are causing the problem; email or talk to their head of year and tutor; and take advice on whether to inform their parents too.

In other words – make this complaint have a useful effect for you. Demonstrating that the bad behaviour of a small group isn't affecting you personally but is damaging the progress of other students, and that their parents have been annoyed enough to raise it, does raise the stakes somewhat and gives you the moral high ground of being seen to tackle the behaviour issue on behalf of students and not just for yourself.

TALKING POINTS

- Who would be the first person you would turn to if you received a complaint like this?
- How would you try to avoid worrying about the complaint?

41 How to respond to a parents' consultation interview that goes badly wrong

Occasionally – very occasionally – a parent interview starts to spin remorselessly out of control. In my experience, this is often based on the parents arriving at the interview with some mistaken perception of a situation. They may have been given an account by their child that is – how should we put this? – not entirely consistent with the truth. They then present this in an overly assertive manner. Here is an example:

> Our daughter says you favour other people in the class and when she puts her hand up to answer questions you ignore her and choose other people instead and you don't mark her work as thoroughly as other people so now she's falling behind and really hates your subject.

They can, of course, go on rather longer, or have complaints about everyone else's behaviour (not of the child of the parents, who is likely to be presented as someone on the waiting list for sainthood), or about marking, or about you not knowing your subject, or homework not being set, or the child being in the wrong group, or a myriad other concerns.

Often, they mask a relationship between the child and parents that has hit problems. My experience suggests that over-assertive parents who are loath to listen to the school's viewpoint on an issue are either being manipulated by their child or are covering up for what they know are his or her shortcomings.

No matter what my cod psychology suggests, you are the one sitting there, and these parents are making life difficult.

So, how do you deal with it?

Well, note first of all that our basic formula for a parental interview gets this issue into the open straight away. You have started your discussion with a handshake, or attempted handshake, and then asked, 'Are there any issues you would like to raise before I tell you how I think Rachel is doing?'

Although that approach invites the parents' criticism right at the start, it is the best way. They will not be able to claim that they have not had a chance to say what they want.

The interview will now depend on how vociferous the parents are, but my strong advice, always, is, let them vent their spleen. Stay calm, listen to what they are saying and, however turbulent your feelings, try not to show them. Instead, if only as a way of channelling your fury or frustration, make a point of writing down the key points of their complaints.

If they are complaining about your abilities as a teacher, then a parents' evening is not the place to start debating it – even if they want to. These events are designed for updating parents on the progress of their child.

So here is how to respond:

Initially, let the parental diatribe flow. That is, let the parents have their say, but not to the extent that it is going to make your next appointment late.

If it is a complaint lasting a minute or two that then comes to an end, you need to give a formal acknowledgement of what has been said, but – I would suggest – do not try to respond to the points they have made in detail. Instead, defer those to a different occasion, when you can meet the parents with your head of department or mentor with you.

Here is the kind of language you might use:

Well, obviously I'm disappointed that Rachel feels that way and that you do too. I see things rather differently, but clearly with just two minutes before my next appointment I'm not going to be able to respond to everything you have complained about. However, I have noted the key points. What I suggest is that we make a separate appointment later this week when we'll go through those points, asking Rachel and my head of department to attend too, and we'll resolve any misunderstandings. That's probably the best we can do. Is that all right? I suggest you either email me or put some possible dates and times in Rachel's homework diary that you could make, and we'll fix the meeting up.

What I'll do for this final minute or so is give you the feedback I had prepared on how I think Rachel is doing. We can discuss it in more detail at the meeting we arrange.

So, in terms of Rachel's progress . . .

Does that all make sense? Once again, I'm sorry you've felt you've had to come with a complaint this evening. We'll resolve it at the next meeting if you send in those suggested times. Now I'll need to see my next parent. Many thanks for coming in.

As ever, you will do this in your own style. Exchanges such as this feel stilted on the page. Let's accept that. But notice what this response does. It:

- acknowledges their interpretation;

- states that you have a different view, but without putting you in the position of justifying or defending yourself in a semi-public forum;

- uses a couple of questions ('Is that all right?'), designed to show you are being conciliatory;

- defers the issue to a time and place when you can (a) have investigated the underlying causes of the complaint, (b) have prepared a response and (c) have someone with you to help ensure that the next meeting is measured and professional;

- reinforces the fact that you are in control of the interview, not the parent.

TALKING POINTS

- What is the most challenging conversation with a parent you have had to deal with so far?
- Which parts of the advice above feel relevant? Which feel impossible?
- What might you do to get some practice for dealing with difficult parental interviews?

WHAT I LOVE ABOUT TEACHING

I really like seeing young people learn and change. You watch them grow up and develop enthusiasms and areas of special interest. You can sometimes see where one comment in one lesson has opened a child's mind to a whole new area of knowledge.

42 How to deal with the most challenging parents at a parents' evening

Brace yourself. Occasionally, these discussions can be much worse, so let's look at how to deal with a more extreme scenario.

This is a parent on a mission, and you sense things are not well from when you proffer your hand at the start of the parental interview and get snubbed. Then it goes like this:

> We've been wanting to see you. My son says he hasn't learned anything since you started teaching him and he can hardly follow what's going on because the discipline is so bad. So we want him moved to another group where he can actually learn something.

With a confrontational opener like this, you will need to use all your emotional resources to stay calm and apparently unflappable (however flapped you may be feeling beneath the surface). As ever, routines can help, so start by asking the parents whether there are some specific concerns they have.

Expect a response like this: 'I've just told you, haven't I? Are you thick or something? I want him moved to another group and I want it to happen now.'

This is where you need to get ready to press the detonator button on this interview, even if it causes a little scene. You could, of course, sit there and let it play out a bit longer, but my view is that there is no reason that any teacher – indeed, any member of staff – should be subjected to an abusive approach such as this. It is the use of the word 'thick' that is most noticeable, of course, but, even without that, this feels to me like an interview that has an underlying sense of contempt that is simply unacceptable.

Here is how to get out of it. And remember, a situation such as this is one where, even if it does provoke a localised, embarrassing drama, it is worth putting down a marker about courtesy and respect.

So, calmly, without a whiff of being patronising, say something like this:

> All right, Mr and Mrs Davis. I'm really not thick, and it's not a word I use. Nor am I in a position to talk about whether Elliot should be in a different group. I'm not going to continue the conversation now but will instead ask Mr X, Head of English, to contact you, and we will discuss Elliot's progress and the group he is in and the teacher he has at a different time.

At this point, you stand up and proffer a hand. There will be some bluster, some disagreement, a bit of a scene. Stand your ground and, as we would with students, deflect this issue from being about the effect on you to being about the effect on other parents – like this: 'As you can see, I have got other parents to see, and it will be better for all of us if we can have a proper, detailed conversation about Elliot more privately'.

If the parents stay there arguing, apologise to the next group of parents by saying: 'Sorry for the inconvenience. I will be with you in a minute. Mr and Mrs Davis, if you will excuse me'.

Then, go and find the senior member of staff who is on duty, or interrupt your head of department by saying, 'Sorry to interrupt, Mr X, but may I just have an urgent word', and then leave it to one of those more highly experienced, more highly paid colleagues to remove the parent from your desk. Then, return, smiling, and say, 'Apologies for the delay. Now – the parents of Suzanne Gaynor please . . .'

Becoming a teacher

Your heart will be racing. You will be feeling woeful. But you have done the right thing. Just as airports and banks and post offices have signs saying, 'We will not tolerate abuse of our staff', there is no reason why you should tolerate treatment like that.

Although it is not pleasant at the time, you will get stronger, emotionally, as a result, and word will spread among parents about what kinds of exchange are appropriate and not. You will have helped to define the ethos.

And, at the very least, you deserve a note of congratulation from your head of department or mentor.

TALKING POINTS

- Can you imagine yourself dealing with a scenario like this?
- Which parts of the advice do you agree with? Which feel remote and unfathomable to you?

43 How to write high quality reports

Whatever your subject, the ability to write clear, accurate English is important. It will enable you to communicate effectively. It is also something on which – like it or not – you will be quietly judged, by parents, by senior staff responsible for checking reports and by colleagues.

That does not mean you have to be a perfectly accurate writer. You may, like lots of us, lack confidence when it comes to putting ideas down on paper. However, there are some simple strategies that are likely to help you to be clear and accurate most of the time.

Here are some suggested strategies:

Know your school's house style

Each school will have a house style – an expectation of the way certain concepts should be consistently expressed. For example, it might be that year groups ('Year 9') always have a capital 'Y' for year. Know this, so that you contribute to the consistency of the school's external messages.

Here are examples of a suggested house style:

- Year 9: capital Y and a number.
- Mathematics/mathematics: upper case for school subject titles; lower case for the concept. So, 'He has worked very

hard in Science and Music this year.' 'It is clear that science and music are the most important interests he has.'

- Sixth Form needs capitals.
- Specific and named clubs and activities need capitals, e.g. Dance Club.

Common errors/spellings

- Do not use capital letters for words such as 'school' or 'university', unless they are part of a named establishment (e.g. Bristol University).
- Do not use capital letters for seasons – 'in the summer examinations . . .'
- It is 'coursework', not 'course work'.
- It is 'homework', not 'home work'.
- It's = it is; its = belonging to it (as in 'the school has its own dedicated student support team').

Hyphens

These seem to cause a great deal of confusion. They are used to link together words when the meaning relies on the link. Here are some examples:

- 'Look at that man eating chicken' – the man is eating chicken.
- 'Look at that man-eating chicken' – the chicken is a man-eater.
- In the forest there are five hundred year old trees (unhyphenated and ambiguous).

Look at the effect of adding hyphens to show links and, therefore, meaning:

- In the forest there are five hundred year-old trees (i.e. five hundred trees, each of which is one year old).

- In the forest there are five hundred-year-old trees (five trees, each of which is a hundred years old).

- In the forest there are five-hundred-year-old trees (some trees that are five hundred years old).

- Note: 'The man is well known' (no hyphen needed, as the word 'well' is simply qualifying the word 'known'.

- But: 'He is a well-known man' (we are not saying that the man is both well and known; the two words must be linked together by the hyphen).

- 'He has spent a great deal of extra curricular time on the project' would mean that he has spent additional curriculum time on it. To signify time outside the curriculum, it needs a hyphen – '*extra-curricular*' time.

Other common phrases used in reports that need hyphens

- End-of-unit tests;
- a well-organised project;
- a well-planned piece of work;
- a good-humoured member of the group;
- he is a hard-working student;
- self-confidence.

Note: Never hyphenate compounds that are created with '-ly' adverbs, even when they come before nouns and act as an adjective:

- He is a quietly spoken person (not 'quietly-spoken').
- It was a badly planned project (not 'badly-planned').

Other common errors

Practice/practise

'Practice' (the noun) and 'practise' (the verb): 'He needs to do some more practice' and 'He needs to practise more frequently'. If in doubt, remember the difference between advice and advise, which it is difficult to get wrong.

However

The word 'however' causes some problems. There are three ways to use it:

- 'However hard he tries he is unlikely to succeed' (no comma).

- 'However, he should not give up, as there is still time to revise' (comma after 'however').

- 'If he works hard, however, he may well surprise us all' (comma before and after 'however').

Commas

Use of commas: these help break up sentences to make the meaning clear, and you can usually tell where they should go if you read the sentence out loud, noting where you naturally pause (as in this sentence).

Do not, however, join up two independent clauses with a comma, as this is the notorious *comma splice*.

 If you find this difficult, the following link contains a useful explanation and some examples to practise: www.bristol.ac.uk/arts/exercises/grammar/grammar_tutorial/page_07.htm

Basic information on writing accurate sentences

The comma splice is one of the most frequent mistakes made when using a comma. It occurs when a comma is used to connect two independent clauses.

In the following example, the two clauses make sense on their own. Connecting them with a comma is incorrect:

> Jim usually gets on with everybody, he is an understanding person.

If you have two independent clauses that need to be separated, you have several choices:

- You can make them into two sentences using a *full stop*. This is probably the easiest solution, but may not be the best in terms of style or developing your argument.

  > Jim usually gets on with everybody. He is an understanding person.

- You can use a *semicolon*. Semicolons should not be overused but can be very powerful when used in the correct situations. In our example, using a semicolon suggests a link between the two clauses without stating that link specifically. This can be a powerful tool in developing a convincing argument.

  > Jim usually gets on with everybody; he is an understanding person.

- You can introduce a *conjunction* to connect the sentences. By doing this, you make the connection between the two more explicit.

  > Jim usually gets on with everybody because he is an understanding person.
  > Jim usually gets on with everybody, as he is an understanding person.

General

- Remember that the report is addressed to the parent not the child. There should be no comments such as, 'Well done, James!' Any targets need to be in the form of 'He needs to . . .' or 'She should try to . . .', rather than being expressed as a direct instruction to the student.

- The report should be intelligible to any parent, so unnecessary jargon or complex language should be avoided. So rather than 'He needs to realise the *gravitas* of these exams', use 'importance'.

- The tone should be professional and formal. Avoid words such as 'incredible' and 'fantastic'; instead, use words such as 'excellent', 'impressive', 'outstanding'.

- Don't make inappropriate personal comments or judgements, for example, 'She is a lovely girl with a cheeky smile'. You might, however, comment on behavioural characteristics, such as reliability and courtesy.

- Ensure that negative/critical comments are based on evidence, do not appear as global judgements ('He is lazy') and are expressed professionally ('On a number of occasions he has failed to complete the work set').

Remember the purpose of reports and the intended audience. We want reports to be characterised by clear, straightforward language that will help parents to know how their children are progressing. Therefore, avoid jargon, acronyms and clichés; write to parents telling them how their daughter or son might develop.

Other aspects of style

- Use *he* or *she* and *his* or *her*, not *you/your.*

- Ensure that comments are *evidence-based* (what the student *has* or *has not* achieved).

- Use simple, *clear language* that will get your message across to parents.

- Make sure you are being *constructive*, even if the student struggles with effort or behaviour; give helpful targets to find a way forward.

- Use *full stops* after all statements.

Remember that this is just one recommended house style. Your school may have a different approach, but the list above at least gives you an outline of some of the language conventions to be aware of and decisions you need to make, if you are to write good-quality reports.

TALKING POINTS

- Does all of this advice make sense?
- How confident are you as a writer?
- Have you read reports by other teachers to help you to see what to do and what not to do?

44 How to avoid common errors when writing reports

Here are some of the most commonly made mistakes in teachers' reports.

- Affect/effect: 'affect' is a verb relating to emotion or pretentiousness/affectation ('The man affects an American accent'; 'he was genuinely affected by the music'); 'effect' is usually a noun ('His arrival had a big effect'), but can be used as a verb meaning to change: 'She effected changes as soon as she was appointed').
- Use 'a lot', not 'alot'.
- Use 'all sorts', not 'alsorts'.
- 'Basically': this word is unnecessary in most contexts.
- Continuous/continual: a continuous noise never stops; a continual noise is frequent but with interruptions.
- Use 'comprises' or 'consists of', but not 'comprises of'.
- Dependant/dependent: a 'dependant' is a noun ('He looked after his dependants'); 'dependent' is an adjective ('They were dependent upon him').
- Use 'different from', not 'different than'.
- 'Discreet' = modest/restrained; 'discrete' = separate.
- 'Disinterested' = neutral/objective; 'uninterested' = not interested.

How to avoid errors when writing reports

- Rather than 'due to', use 'because of'.

- 'Every day' = noun and adverb ('It happens every day'); everyday = adjective ('an everyday remark').

- 'Formally' = being formal; 'formerly' = in the past.

- Use 'fraction' with care: saying 'he only produced a fraction of the necessary work' is not the same as saying 'a small fraction', as 9/10 is a fraction.

- 'Homogeneous' = of the same kind; 'homogenous' = of common descent.

- Imply/infer: I imply that you are mad; you infer that I am being rude.

- 'It's' = it is/it has; 'its' – the cat licked its paws.

- Like: use 'as if' ('It looks as if he will be late').

- 'Led' = past tense of to lead; 'lead' = rope for a dog and heavy element.

- Less/fewer: use 'less' for quantities ('I'll have less water'); use 'fewer than' for items that can be individually counted ('fewer than ten bottles').

- Literally: use with care; not 'He literally jumped out of his skin'.

- Use 'meet', not 'meet with'.

- Momentarily: 'He stopped momentarily', not the Americanism, 'I'll be there momentarily'.

- 'More than' is better than 'over' ('It cost more than £27').

- Use 'no one', not 'no-one'.

- 'Onto' doesn't exist. The phrase is 'on to'.

- 'Prevaricate' = to lie or deceive; 'procrastinate' = to put something off.

- 'Principal' = head of a school; 'principle/principles' = beliefs.

- 'Program' – runs on a computer; 'programme' – something we watch on television or buy at a theatre.

Becoming a teacher

- Theirs (no apostrophe).
- Use 'try to', not 'try and'.
- Use 'under way', not 'underway'.
- Use 'until', not 'up until'.
- 'Upcoming': avoid.
- Use 'while', not 'whilst'.
- Yours (no apostrophe).
- Use 'outside', not 'outside of'.

TALKING POINTS

- Are there any of these that don't make sense?
- Are there any that surprise you?

WHAT I LOVE ABOUT TEACHING

The little successes - the occasional thank-you notes - and the holidays. All of these make teaching a really special job.

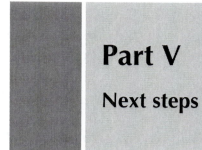

Part V

Next steps

Teaching practice was about learning techniques, approaches and routines. It is about getting some things right and some things wrong, preferably more of the former than the latter.

Watch as many teachers teaching as you can. Note how they manage a group, ask questions and give instructions; how they explain and how they know when to pause; look at how they manage question-and-answer sessions with students. Look at their marking and their planning and listen to their conversations with students.

Try to keep doing this through your career, getting into other people's classrooms and tutor rooms. Learn from the veterans.

A great teacher will be able to deliver very high quality lessons over and over. They won't all, of course, be perfect. We are not robots.

However, there will be a level of consistency from one lesson to the next – in expectations, routines, use of praise and marking – that makes you feel that this teacher could help any student to achieve his or her best.

As their confidence grows, these teachers contribute more to the school, through work with colleagues and through greater involvement in the life of the school.

This short chapter explores this phase of your career, including looking at where you may head next.

45 You're a teacher

What were you worrying about?

Congratulations, as you move to the end of your training, or prepare to take up your first teaching post – you made it. I hope that, as you look back over the months of your training, you can see how you have developed professionally and as a person. Teaching is an extraordinary job for exposing us to who we are – to what we know, how well we know it, how we speak, how we interact with others and suchlike.

For those of us who are thin-skinned, it can therefore be a job that brings huge and obsessive levels of self-doubt. That, in my experience, never entirely goes away. We lose sleep before new school years, new terms and, in some cases, before new weeks.

We develop a kind of remorseless absorption with 'Was my lesson good enough?', 'Why did this bit work but not that?', 'How could I teach this topic better?' and 'Will they behave for me?' – these kinds of question often stalk even the most apparently self-confident of teachers.

Accept it. Recognise that it is this level of reflectiveness, of forensic self-criticism that keeps driving the best teachers to get better.

Then, have strategies for dealing with the worry. Have things you do that take you away from your desk, from your marking, from the punishing sense that your work will never be complete.

Next steps

Do not allow yourself to spend all weekends working for the school week ahead. Build in time away from your computer, away from your piles of books. Make one day each weekend a work-free zone and use it to go somewhere – meet friends, see a film, go into the countryside, escape your worries.

It is important that you do this. We need great teachers, not great but neurotic ones.

We opened this book with a series of real life worries expressed by trainee teachers. Here we return to them, to make sure that all of those early concerns have been dealt with.

What happens if I walk into a classroom and they all laugh at me?

They won't. Why would they? Dress and conduct yourself in a way that establishes you firmly as part of the school culture, and you will benefit from the authority given to you by being part of the ethos. Play the part of a teacher. Greet students as they arrive at your lesson. Establish your expectations about where they sit, what equipment they need and suchlike as they enter, so that, even before you address the class as a full group, the students know that you are purposeful and organised.

Is there a good way to increase my confidence?

Confidence comes from controlling as many of the controllable elements as possible. It also comes from routines and practice. These elements give us a sense of familiarity.

So plan as much as you can in advance, to minimise the risks of things going wrong. In your earliest lessons, do not plan anything too experimental or too reliant on technology. Use this early phase to establish yourself as a teacher that students want to be taught by, someone who is clear and purposeful, who knows their stuff and can explain it, who is approachable, but takes no nonsense.

Preparation means:

- getting to know the rooms you will be teaching in;

- customising the room, where possible, to reflect your expectations, expressed through displays; this establishes an underlying sense of your values and approach; have a teacher's desk that is tidy and uncluttered and exudes a sense of calm purpose;

- planning a lesson that has a broad, logical arc to it: a clear overall structure where you know the shape of what students will learn and the activities that will lead to this; such a sense of reassuring clarity will help you to teach a confident lesson;

- knowing the background information about the students you are teaching;

- having a back-up for any part of the lesson that might go wrong; I'm writing this on a day when I've watched four lessons in another school: in two of them, the interactive whiteboard didn't work, and the teachers struggled. Be gloomy: assume technology will fail and have a plan B.

Are there any easy ways of learning names?

Use your first lesson to make a seating plan. Take the register explicitly and publicly in every lesson and, in the early days, get students to put up their hands when their name is called: use this moment to say hello and to match the name with a face.

Print off a class list that includes photographs of the students (if these are already on the school system) and spend five minutes at home or between lessons practising learning names. It gets easier, the longer you teach.

What are the best things to write in my personal statement before applying?

Three suggestions:

- Include anything that shows your suitability as a teacher – especially experience of teaching, coaching, volunteering, supervising others. Make explicit roles of responsibility.

- Include anything that highlights your sense of character and your qualities of reliability and trustworthiness.

- Show your commitment to teaching, your understanding of what the job entails and your willingness to learn.

What is the best way to design a worksheet?

Worksheets are the bread and butter of teaching. They can provoke a sense of heart-sinking gloom in students, because all too often they appear to be designed to fill time, to keep a class occupied. They also get forgotten, ripped, lost and abandoned, thereby undermining any shred of authority they might have had as a tool for learning.

So use worksheets sparingly, as necessary, and insist that students stick them neatly into a folder or exercise book as part of their homework. At the start of the next lesson, check that this has happened and, if it hasn't, ask the student to write a reminder to do so in their planner or homework diary, and ask that they see you next day to demonstrate that they have done this. Then make a note in your own diary of this arrangement.

Worksheets – like so many other aspects of being a teacher – carry a kind of symbolism: they demonstrate your standards and expectations. If you give the worksheet status, then, in the eyes of students, it will have status.

In terms of designing an effective worksheet, here are some suggestions:

- Be clear what you are designing it for: what are students expected to learn as a result of using it?

- Then, design it with the student in mind, grabbing attention at the start (e.g. visually, through a picture, and big question).

- Demystify any important vocabulary through a boxed glossary near the start of the worksheet (i.e. let students encounter the difficult words before they begin reading the text).

- Use questions in the margins during a lengthy text to build students' confidence in understanding it.

- Use a font style and size that increase accessibility (not Comic Sans, not smaller than 12 point).

- Have white space on the handout – don't clutter it with text and images.

- Collect some samples of effective handouts during your teaching practice: look at how simple good visuals can make a complex subject interesting, attractive and more accessible.

How do I write a lesson plan?

There is a detailed section on this topic on page 62. As you become more experienced, lesson planning will become more intuitive and less time-consuming. In the early days, it can feel crushingly intrusive. These are my three main tips:

1   Build lesson plans around learning rather than activities. That means being forensically clear about what you want students to know and be able to do at the end of a year, term, unit of work or lesson. It means knowing what the students will need to be able to do to demonstrate their learning (for example, what they will have to say, write, make or perform). Learning should drive the sequence of activities you plan.

2   It follows from this that you should start at the end of the lesson and work back. And be ambitious – what do you want *every* student to know and do, not just some?

3   Remember that great lesson plans don't translate into great lessons. Great lessons arise from how you adapt your planning to the needs of the students in front of you. That will mean sometimes dwelling for longer on an activity than you had planned, or changing direction because the class already knows more than you had anticipated. A lesson plan is a plan, not a recipe.

How open can I be with students about my own belief (religious or political)?

This one depends on context.

Teachers sometimes think that students are more interested in our private lives, backgrounds and beliefs than they actually are. In general, in most lessons in most subjects, you won't refer at all to your life out of school.

However, it may be that, as a tutor, or in a class discussion, you are asked about your beliefs – political or religious – or simply for a point of view about something in the news or that happened in a television programme the night before.

My advice is to tread carefully. First, you don't want to develop a reputation as a teacher who is easily deflected from the lesson in hand, someone whom students enjoy nudging to talk about stuff they think might be more interesting than your planned lesson.

Second, you don't want to open yourself to accusations of moving beyond professional boundaries, to talking with students about any topic that is personal.

On the other hand, students sometimes need us, as adults, to help them to navigate a complex and difficult world. We want to show that, as adult members of society, there are things we believe are important – family, belief in something, voting and suchlike.

Therefore, if asked, it is not unreasonable to give a short answer, such as this one:

Student: So are you political? Would you vote for the government?

Me: Good question. We haven't got time for me to talk in detail, and in any case it's developing *your* views that's important. But, yes, I do believe in voting. I believe it was a right, a freedom that was won for us by people in the past, and that we have a duty to vote. Other people would disagree, but I think voting is important. As to who I would vote for, well that's something I keep to myself. Now, back to the topic.

You will see that the answer is slightly oblique: it avoids giving away anything too personal, or anything that could lead to accusations of being partisan or unprofessional.

I would recommend that, if you find that a discussion does go off in a direction such as this one, you follow the advice above, but also cover yourself by explaining to your mentor or head of department what you were asked and how you responded: this is a useful safety net that shows that you are aware of the potential risks of talking from more personal experience.

What happens if I don't have a pigeonhole?

As a trainee teacher, you won't have a pigeonhole. You won't need one. Be grateful. Soon enough, as a teacher, you will often look back and wish you didn't have one either.

While you are a trainee, people will pass the notes and information you need via your mentor or someone else you work with; more likely, any non-spoken communication will be done via email.

Then, as a teacher, you will know you have truly got a foothold in the profession: you will have been allocated a pigeonhole, one of those curious icons that mark out the school staffroom from the rest of the school.

Pigeonholes can be a curse, for you and the person passing material on to you, because they can become clogged with notes, letters, odd exercise books and suchlike. For you, you will lose the sense of what is new and what has been there for ages. For the person posting to it, there will be frustration that messages passed on to you never get looked at.

So aim to clear your pigeonhole, when you have one, twice a day. Go to work via the staffroom and on an explicit mission to keep it empty. Whatever is in there – take it with you. Refuse to let your lazier self leave anything in there. Be an exemplar of the decluttered life. Then, take any notes and messages and, as quickly as possible, deal with them. If there are notes to contact someone – say, to call a parent of someone in your tutor group, or to send work for an absent student via email to a head of year – then either sit down and do it straight away, or have a notebook in which you list the administrative tasks for the day ahead. Note the message and any essential details it contains and then physically throw away the paper. Enjoy the catharsis of getting rid of miscellaneous papers.

In other words, you have a single choice: act immediately on the message and throw it away, or note it on that day's to-do list and throw it all away.

There will be other stuff in your pigeonhole that will, if you let it, accumulate – flyers, general information and junk mail. Throw it away. If you accidentally throw away something that proves later to be important, then whoever sent it will get back in touch with you.

As with email, don't be a slave to your pigeonhole: you control it. In a profession such as teaching, it is one of the most satisfying areas of controlling time and space that we have.

Will there be coffee on tap?

Probably not. Don't get too reliant on coffee, and certainly never have a cup of tea or coffee that you drink while teaching, in front of students. I have never known a good teacher who would see this as anything other than discourteous or self-indulgent.

Tea and coffee are for break and lunchtimes, not to punctuate the teaching of a lesson.

But do drink lots of water. Have a bottle of water on the go in your classroom all day.

What should I wear on my first day?

Dress in a way that shows you are a member of a profession that exemplifies high standards. Dress in a way that is more smart than casual, in which there is a degree of formality.

The way you dress will send out a message about what you expect from students. If you are teaching in something casual or unkempt, students will infer that you have lower expectations. Of course, there are great teachers who dress in a way that is pretty informal, but chances are they are established teachers: their reputations have been forged by word-of-mouth, through hundreds of lessons.

You, on the other hand, are starting out. You are untried and untested. All the research on teacher effectiveness tells us that students make very accurate judgements, very quickly, about the quality of a teacher.

The way you open the door, the way you take the register, the way you say 'Hello': all of these will count towards the initial assessment students make of your abilities.

They will have begun to make their decision before you say a word. Where you stand as they arrive, how you stand and – crucially – how you look: all of these matter.

So, on that important first day, don't leave the way you dress to chance. Dress deliberately. If in doubt about whether to be slightly more casual or more formal, default to the formal option.

What do I do if a student tells me something personal about their background – e.g. that they are being abused?

Say, straight away, something like, 'Look – I'm glad you've told me this, but I'm going to have to tell a more senior member of staff.

Next steps

What you've told me worries me, and it's important that you get all the support you need.'

Whatever the student says, however he or she begs you not to tell, you need, as soon as possible, to go and see the school's designated safeguarding officers – the senior staff who are directly responsible for issues of child protection.

If they are in a meeting, ask someone to interrupt it.

What you must not do is ignore what you have been told, or keep it to yourself, or be pressurised not to pass it on. The child may – whether he or she admits it or not – need help urgently. It is your responsibility to make sure that the message is passed on.

What should I expect at a job interview?

There is detail about this on page 154, but the essence of our advice is:

- apply carefully;
- remember that you are being judged throughout the day, and not just when teaching a sample lesson or being interviewed;
- use the day to see if the school is right for you;
- answer questions by giving examples, where possible, from your experience;
- dress smartly, smile and don't talk too much.

How long is it likely to be before I will be teaching unsupported?

That will vary from school to school and according to the progress in your classroom practice that you are perceived to be making.

It is a good question, because the reality of learning to teach, indeed of learning most things, is that there comes a point when you need to be left alone (well, alone with twenty-five or more young people) to know how it really feels and how you are really doing.

If you are getting confident and feeling constrained by a mentor or other teacher at the back of the group, discuss it. Ask to be given more opportunities to teach the class without an observer.

It may be that the school is resistant; indeed, it may be that you have asked before you are actually ready, but it is worth asking if the quantity of observation is proving oppressive.

What happens if I don't like/can't work with/fancy my mentor?

This happens – at least the first two elements in the question do.

They are bound to – just as there will be people on your training course, and perhaps in your own family, with whom you would rather not mix, so it will be in school.

The level of whether it is a real issue or not rather depends upon you. If it is someone whose manner you don't like – say, he is too nit-picking, too critical, too serious, too pompous – then it may be that this is just the person you need. Sometimes, someone who is most definitely not our preferred choice of guide or mentor does us good, forces us to reflect, keeps us on our toes.

In any case, training to teach will always be stressful, and you need to be careful that an apparently unhappy relationship with your mentor isn't just an indication of deeper and understandable anxiety about the school, the training, the job.

So give it some time before you decide whether the relationship is dysfunctional. If you really think it is not working, or that it is impeding your progress as a teacher, then you will need to talk to someone else. This might be your PGCE tutor back at the university, or the senior member of staff in the school who has responsibility for teacher training.

You will need to present the issue carefully and sensitively, perhaps saying something like this:

> I'm really sorry to have to bring this issue to you but after a lot of thought I feel I need to. It's my relationship with my mentor.

It's just not working, and it's having the effect of making me lose sleep and feel even more stressed about my teaching.

I have noted down precisely what the problem is and hope that you might be able to resolve it for me.

It might be that something constructive can be done; it might be that it can't. It might, therefore, be that you are stuck with the person assigned to you as mentor, and that a difficult conversation ensues when he asks why you complained about him.

That, however, is a risk you will need to think about, and there is a response:

It wasn't a complaint about you. It was me saying that I find it difficult to work with you. I'm aware that you have mentored many people in the past and your track-record is very good. But in my case I have to say that it's not really working and I felt it only right to mention this to XX. I didn't really know how I could broach it with you so, after a lot of thought, I decided I would see whether there was any possibility of being mentored by someone else.

But, as I say, it wasn't a complaint about you, just a sign that I felt I needed a different kind of support. So – I'm sorry if you felt undermined by my request, but it was done with my best intentions.

A frosty tone may characterise further meetings, but you should smile, be positive, remain professional and do your best to work with this mentor.

And, on the other hand, things might get better.

The last part of the question was, 'What if I fancy my mentor?' The answer to this one is simple: don't.

What happens if I get lost?

Expect to.

You ought to be given a map of the school. Grab some time on your own to wander and to get your bearings. Get in early enough each day or stay a bit later in that first week, so that you can wander the school and orientate yourself, without too many students around.

If you do get lost, the best plan is to stop a student and say: 'Excuse me, I've forgotten how to get to the Science area. Could you remind me of the route? Thank you.'

Students will invariably point you in the right direction.

What should I do when I hit the wall/get stuck/get weighed down by too much work?

This will happen. You will hit a trough of terrible gloom and, perhaps, start losing sleep over your abilities or the likely behaviour of a class.

This is a normal part of the job, even for seasoned veterans. You will need someone you can offload on – someone happy to listen patiently to your anxieties.

Also make sure you get out. Try to have one evening during the week – say Wednesday night – when you go out with friends, or take some exercise, or see a film. Do the same at weekends – have one day when you get away from the burgeoning planning and marking.

If things are more serious than a blip of overtiredness, talk to someone at your university department or in the school. Don't keep your worries suppressed. Share them and you will immediately gain a sense that you aren't the first to feel this way. We all did. Many of us still do.

What happens if students try to contact me on Facebook?

This is an important question. Increasingly, as a headteacher, I have to attend to issues that have been caused by staff forgetting about professional boundaries. Keep applying the *Daily Mail* test' that I refer to on page 94: 'Would I be happy for this message to be printed on the front page of the *Daily Mail*?' If there is any uncertainty, then do not send or post the message.

On a day on which the school might be closed because of snow, this includes writing on a Facebook page, 'Hooray – a snow day'. A friend might laugh. A parent is likely to be infuriated, and it is a message that could spiral into an accusation of undermining the reputation of the school. Be careful.

How can I rapidly increase my salary?

Schools have increasing flexibility over pay decisions. They can, from the outset, pay you an additional sum decided by them as part of a 'recruitment' point. If you are exceptional, and they want to keep you at the school, you could receive a 'retention' point, again at a sum fixed by the school. Once you are established as a good teacher, your annual salary will be subject to decisions by the headteacher and governors about increases. These will be linked to your performance and will be reviewed annually as part of the school's appraisal process.

You are free to ask about the possibility of such additional payments at interview, though you will want to get the tone right and, I would suggest, want to avoid appearing to suggest that you will only accept the job if a recruitment point is forthcoming.

It may be that you get towards the end of the interview and are asked whether you have any questions. This is your time to ask, if you wish:

> As you know I'm teaching in a shortage subject and I have a number of other interviews lined up. I hope you don't mind me mentioning this, but I wondered whether you would consider whether I would be paid a recruitment point if I was offered the post here and accepted it? It's something that I feel I should raise with you.

Some candidates would feel uncomfortable raising such an issue; others would be happy to be rather more brazen. This is how I would introduce it – in a spirit of quiet and respectful inquisitiveness, rather than in-your-face self-interest. Good luck.

What happens if I train in a really good school with no behaviour issues and then get a job in a school with lots of behaviour issues?

The same principles apply in all schools:

- set out clear expectations of how students should conduct themselves;

- understand that the key to effective classroom management is being pre-emptive – spotting potential problems before they occur, changing the pace and direction of a lesson just before students' general interest wanes, circulating around the room;

- model the behaviour you expect (i.e. always be polite and calm, however pressured you may be feeling);

- understand that interesting lessons will minimise many behaviour issues;

- insist on silence when you or someone else is speaking publicly;

- use the school's rewards system a lot and its sanctions system as necessary, but not more than necessary (in other words, don't get a reputation as someone who is constantly putting students in detentions and suchlike).

You will encounter some level of behaviour challenge in any school: it is in the nature of teenagers that they will sometimes speak out of turn, be defiant, get upset, feel hemmed in, trapped in a situation they cannot get out of. Don't expect dutiful paragons of virtue, even if you are teaching in the leafiest school, with an Ofsted rating of 'uber-excellent' for its behaviour.

Next steps

Teaching practice is when you hammer out those principles and hone your approach. Then you customise them for the other schools in which you teach.

One of the striking and unexpected aspects is that, whatever stage we are at in our career, we end up having to reassert those principles and that practice every time we move school. I remember being surprised by this when I became a deputy headteacher. I assumed that students would fall into meek compliance at the sight of my pin-striped suit and shimmering name badge. Not a bit.

So – wherever you go, and whatever the school – you will need to deploy your classroom management skills from the outset. That is why, on teaching practice, you should take every opportunity to practise and hone them, and also to watch a range of teachers, in a variety of subjects at work. Watch those who weave a magic sense of invisible behaviour management through their school-based reputation, probably established over many years. Watch those who aren't natural authority figures, who haven't earned their behaviour management stripes through teaching a previous generation of youngsters. These are the ones who use techniques, who set out expectations, who deploy the school's disciplinary codes.

Watch them, talk to them and learn from them.

Then do your very best, at whatever school you work in. Shrug off any talk of the reputation of the school, a particular class or a student for particularly bad behaviour. Assume all will present you with decent behaviour and know what to do when it isn't like that.

When you do have bad moments, bad lessons, bad days and bad weeks, remember that this is normal. It happens to all of us – at every stage of our career. It is what happens in this often exciting, occasionally infuriating and always fascinating career called teaching.

What happens if my mentor makes lots of mistakes in subject knowledge?

A good question, if an unnerving one. I think you should play this situation according to context. It is not your job to train teachers such as your mentor to be better teachers. Your priority is to become a great teacher yourself.

However, it may be that there is a way of approaching the issue without splintering your relationship with your mentor. For example, if the gap in subject knowledge becomes exposed when you are watching him or her teach, then it is something you might want to follow up when discussing the lesson. Your discussion could go something like this:

> You know when you explained to the students about the meaning of 'nadir' saying it was a 'high point' in history, I always thought it was the opposite – a low-point. Have I got it wrong or did I mishear what you said?

It might be, on the other hand, that you don't want to say anything at all – that it is only going to cause tension between you and your mentor, leaving you seeming as if you are the cocky new know-it-all who dares to question the veteran mentor.

So, for now, don't feel on a mission to change the world. Say something about the blunder if the time feels right, and you can formulate a sensitive way of doing so. Otherwise, leave it.

What should I do if my subject knowledge isn't good enough?

This question expresses a familiar concern that, even if it doesn't arise publicly too often, haunts our dreams. Do we really know our subject?

In 1770, the poet Oliver Goldsmith published 'The Deserted Village', which contained this line about the village schoolmaster:

> And still they gaz'd and still the wonder grew,
> That one small head could carry all he knew.

Here was a teacher who seemed to know everything.

On teaching practice, and in our early years, we can encounter lots of teachers like this. They can prove quite intimidating, leaving us feeling not only that we don't know anywhere near as much as they do, but also that we never will.

It is especially easy for all of us, when we are training, to be bewitched by the apparent expertise of the seasoned, established teacher.

'How will we ever know everything that they know?', we ask ourselves.

The reality is that, as young teachers, we often feel intellectually inferior. Modern degree courses inevitably compartmentalise knowledge. We learn bits of a subject, but we can't possibly learn everything.

We know what we know.

So let's just accept this. At the start of your career, you can hardly expect to know what someone halfway through or towards the end will know.

However, if we are serious as teachers, then we will know that teaching is a career in which we keep learning things, in which we model to our students that learning isn't confined to classrooms and driven by the need to pass examinations, but something we all do because knowing things and being able to do things are important and enjoyable.

In other words: relax. Of course there will be aspects, many of them, of your subject that you don't know a lot about.

But one of the joys of teaching is being able to learn things. And the way we know that we have really learned things is by being able to teach them.

All these years on, it is the part of the job that most excites me – being asked a question I don't know the answer to and having to say, 'Great question – I have no idea. But let's find out'.

That is what real teaching and learning should be about.

What do I do to deal with an unfortunate surname in my first few lessons?

This happens – but not very often. And it is not so different from having to learn how to pronounce an unfamiliar first name.

My suggestion is that the first lesson with a class always contains an opening sequence in which you go through the register, adding names to your seating plan and asking students how they pronounce their names and how they want to be known (for example, Florence may prefer you to call her Flo).

If the issue is a funny or embarrassing surname, the chances are you will rarely use it – you will be addressing students by their first name on most occasions.

The main thing is to get the names on to your seating plan, so that, thereafter, you can learn the first names and, in most cases, not have to refer to the surname at all.

What if a lesson goes really badly and kids think I am rubbish – how do I ever overcome this impression?

It is easy to obsess about this – to feel that you have 'lost it' with a group, or that they sense you are not very good. We can spend far too much time lying awake and fretting about this. It is one of those teacherly emotions that recurs throughout your career – the feeling that, with some groups – usually one each year, in my experience – we have lost our touch.

Then we start to think that we will never regain that group's confidence. That, at least, is how the thought patterns can go in those dark, early hour periods of misery.

In my experience, every new lesson gives us something of a fresh start. We need to recalibrate our own mindset and treat the beginning of the next lesson with a group as a new and optimistic opportunity.

Be at the door. Smile. Be crisp and purposeful. Quickly recap the last lesson, get the register done and set the pace for this lesson.

Sometimes, it might be worth acknowledging that the last lesson wasn't great. This can, in my experience, have the effect of clearing the air – like this: 'Last lesson wasn't brilliant, was it? I think I was

209

in a bad mood and you found it hard to concentrate. So let's have a fresh start.'

This kind of approach has worked well for me. Students have found it disarming. It acknowledges that sometimes lessons go well and sometimes they don't – and that the reasons for that can rest on both sides.

The main thing, I would suggest, is to try not to worry about what students may be thinking – first, because they may actually not be thinking that at all (yours, after all, is just one lesson in a seemingly endless sequence of lessons) and, even if they are, then you can't control that.

Worry instead about what you can control. Plan a great next lesson. Muster all your optimism. Then – sock it to them.

How do I find the line between professional and friendly?

You can be both. Always remember that you are there to teach students, not to be their friend. But that isn't the same as not being friendly.

Most important in all of this is having clear professional boundaries and always thinking about any situations that might be misinterpreted. Some of this is common sense. So, if you are meeting a student of either gender one to one to discuss work, then you should be in a room that has a window in it or where the door is left open. You should, in other words, make sure you are not in a situation where you might be open to allegations of improper conduct.

If you have encouraged students to send you work or ask questions by email, then make sure you are following your school's ICT guidance to the letter. That is likely to include using a school, not a personal, email address and possibly copying in your head of department or someone else when replying or sending messages.

Being friendly with students will mean being approachable, giving advice, listening to concerns about their progress in your subject. As soon as you sense that things might be moving into other territory – such as a student wanting to tell you about problems at home – then you need to make clear that you cannot keep any information confidential and that you will have to refer their comments on to someone else.

This is a crucial ingredient in making sure you get the boundaries right, from the very beginning of your career, and that you are exemplifying the distinction between professional and friendly.

How can I develop my teaching skills outside the classroom?

You will become a better teacher if you don't confine your own learning to the classroom. Taking part in extra-curricular activities, accompanying trips and visits, getting involved in teacher research projects, helping with a school production – all of these will prove personally fulfilling as well as professionally instructive.

Too many teachers see their students, and the school they work in, purely through the lens of their own classroom. These are the students they teach, in the subject they teach, in the place where they teach. They don't get to see those same students doing other things – performing in a dance show, playing an instrument, participating in a debate, being put under pressure on a Duke of Edinburgh's Award expedition and suchlike.

It can feel sometimes as if your whole life is being given to the school, but the rewards are considerable – not least the pleasure your students will take in seeing you in the audience at a school concert or other event.

All of these will deepen your understanding of the culture of schools and the way what happens outside the classroom – the school's ethos – can contribute to students' achievement within the classroom.

You are also more likely to feel an affinity with the school, to develop a stronger sense of belonging to its community.

All of this can only be beneficial to your teaching.

Next steps

If it is specifically your own teaching skills you want to develop, then taking time to observe teachers of other subjects – including those that you consider far removed from your own in content and approach – can be eminently helpful.

You don't, after all, need to see whole lessons. Sometimes, observing how another teacher kick-starts a lesson, manages a group discussion, arranges a practical activity, steps back so that students are given more responsibility, or oversees the transitions between lesson elements – all of these can help you to analyse the aspects of teaching that people can find hardest to master.

It may be that the school has teacher learning communities or study groups or research projects. Again, these will get you mixing with other teachers, of subjects beyond your own and experience different from yours. Being open to new approaches and ideas is a hallmark of great teachers. Set the habit early on.

What should I wear in school?

The school will have a dress code. Follow it and – in general – stick to it. If you deviate, be slightly more formal in how you dress rather than more informal. It sets the tone for your teaching. See the advice on page 199.

How can I write effective learning objectives?

The mania for learning objectives appears to be abating. It had started to become something of a formula and, at its worst, would set a madcap notion of three mini-objectives – what 'all, most and some' students were expected to achieve by the end of the lesson.

This is a pretty crude way of trying to build in differentiation and it immediately legitimises failure to achieve by some students.

The main mistake in setting objectives is that teachers too often focus on what they want students to be able to 'do' by the end of a lesson, rather than what they want them to learn.

Be laser-like in this: what are the skills and knowledge that are essential if students are to make progress? Then think what they will have to be able to do in order to demonstrate these to you.

Often, your written learning objective will be brief: 'Learn how to build a powerful argument in a speech' or 'Understand why the Battle of the Somme proved a turning point in Britain's perception of World War I'.

You will probably want to have this on display. You will then want to explain it, possibly using a big question or some other 'hook' to capture students' interest.

Thus in a lesson on persuasive techniques you might say:

> Do you reckon you could be persuaded to do something or say something or think something that you currently don't believe? Are you easily persuaded, or do you believe you can resist pressure from anyone?
>
> So, if you were in a supermarket buying a can of soft drink, would you be happy to buy and be seen with the supermarket's own brand? Or would you go for the famous brand, even if it was a bit more expensive?
>
> How persuadable are you, and how good at persuading?
>
> Take a look at our objective for this lesson. That tells you what I'm expecting all of you to be able to do by the end of the lesson.
>
> The idea is that we are going to explore the skills needed in a speech to persuade our audience to believe what we want them to believe, not what they were expecting.
>
> Let's start by looking at some speeches.

As ever, this will feel a bit hokey on the page. We all have our own speech patterns and ways of phrasing ideas. But it demonstrates the concept of using a big question, a challenge or a problem to be solved to hook our students and then to relate this to the skills or knowledge that they will develop.

How do we keep a work–life balance?

Teaching is a job of rhythms and cycles. There will be some points in the year – in the week, perhaps – that are significantly more stressful than others. 'Work–life balance' should not be taken as meaning that these pressure points can be eliminated, which the shape of a day or week or year can be flattened out into something smooth and bland.

Better is to recognise when those likely stress points occur and to have strategies to cope with them. The start of a new school year, for example, although it can be a shock to the system after an extensive break, is often a time with fewer after-school meetings and other commitments. This is a time to get some of your longer-term planning done and to make time for reading around and beyond your subject. It is a time, while the weather is decent, to make sure you are getting serious time off at weekends and at least one evening off a week.

Then, there will be the cluster of parents' evenings, the hefty weight of report writing, the mock examinations that need marking. As we get tired and, more crucially, as students get tired, these are the points in the year when the darkening nights and intensifying pressure can make the job seem much, much tougher and potentially unmanageable.

This is where you have to be firm with yourself, compartmentalising work into what is essential, desirable and less important. It is when some of your more ambitious ideas for lessons – the heavily time-consuming ones – may need to be postponed.

Instead, focus on planning and teaching solid, effective lessons, but cut down the risks of failure. In the toughest parts of the school year, you don't want to spook yourself with a succession of lessons that don't go well. Look for ways of reducing your marking load – increase the amount of peer assessment, build in lesson-based periods when you are seeing students one-to-one or in small groups to talk through your feedback.

Most importantly, don't allow the pressure of the job to hem in your life unnecessarily. Insist on getting out for an evening of non-teacher talk, or to see a film, or to go for a Sunday walk, or meeting friends, or heading home.

Actively make time for yourself and don't feel guilty about it. Recognise also that there will be times when reclaiming a true, long-term sense of work–life balance may need to wait until the next half-term break: sometimes, it will be a case of just pushing on through the tougher times, until you reach the more tranquil spots of time ahead.

What do I do if I get flustered in front of a class? Or, even worse, get emotional?

Teaching has an element of performance. Sometimes, we have to pretend to be more annoyed about something than we actually are. Or we need to pretend to be more interested in a student's response. And sometimes – quite often, in fact – we have to pretend to be calmer than we are actually feeling.

We all know that feeling that, under the surface, we are getting wound up. We can sense the physical sensations emerging. We know that, if we are not careful, we are going to say something or do something that we will regret.

That is when you need to have some form of autopilot – of being able to suppress your natural instinct to say something sarcastic or nasty or to allow yourself to get emotional.

If necessary, detonate a kind of destruct button. If the lesson isn't working, students are proving challenging, and you can feel that you are going to end up losing your self-control, bail out. Say to the class, 'Pens down everyone. This isn't working properly. I'm not happy with the way it's going. We're therefore changing direction for the rest of the lesson.'

Sometimes, this form of explicit acknowledgement that there is a problem can change the emotional temperature of the lesson. It can come as an unexpected relief to the class and take the pressure off you – chiefly because it reasserts you as the authority in the room, rather than that growing sense that the students are setting the agenda.

If things are getting very difficult, and you can feel that you are not coping, then you need to get out of the lesson. If there is another teacher or your head of department next door, send a reliable student to get him or her and say you need to leave the lesson and that you will explain later.

It is rare to have to do this, but, if you need to, then do it. Someone else senior to you will take responsibility for covering the lesson.

You will then feel guilty and will start to worry about what your class will think when you return next lesson. Do not worry; instead, be ready to smile, say hello and say, 'Sorry I didn't feel very well in the last lesson and had to leave in a hurry. I'm fine now. So here goes'.

Turn on the autopilot, play the role of teacher and just motor on.

Make sure you have got some sympathetic people – for example, your mentor or a friend in another school – to whom you can talk and listen. In the darkest days of teaching, we need people to share the experiences with. They sustain us and give us a much-needed sense of camaraderie.

How do I deal with violence (in the classroom or at break time)?

Whatever you may read in the media, most schools are an oasis of calm. Violence is rare. Although, inevitably, there will be flare-ups, when the hormones and frustrations of teenagers spill over into school life, these will be rare.

Your classroom will be all the more calm if you set clear expectations and insist on some very basic rules of respect and courtesy – for example, no student ever being allowed to speak while you or someone else is speaking; all students having coats off and bags on the floor; an insistence that work must be completed neatly. Much of this stuff – the low-level obsession with details – sets a tone that prevents bigger issues arising.

If you do come across violence or aggression, you will need to respond. It may be that you are out on duty and you see trouble brewing. Send a student to get some support from Reception, emphasising that it is urgent. Walk over to where the incident is and ask spectators to leave and those in the middle of it to separate. Ask them to stand apart and, if you can, take them to an office or other place where the issue can be dealt with quietly, rather than in front of an audience.

It is not that you will need to do the follow-up to resolve the issue, but rather that you should try to calm the situation down by moving those involved somewhere else.

Occasionally – very occasionally, in my experience – tempers are so heated that a fight has begun, and, if it is safe for you to do so, you may want to break it up, to try to separate the people involved.

If you are in a school where this kind of event happens, then it is likely that duty staff will wear fluorescent jackets, carry radios and be on duty in greater numbers. There ought to have been training for staff before they go on duty.

Remember that this worst-case stuff is rare: in most situations, your role will be to have some stern words with students, reduce the potential for physical conflict and leave the scenario as calm as you can, ready for someone more experienced to deal with.

Early on in your training, spend some time with a seasoned member of the duty staff. Walk around with him or her. Look at how situations are dealt with, quiet conversations are held and potential conflicts are skilfully pre-empted.

TALKING POINTS

- Do these questions cover everything you have been wondering about?
- Do you have any more to add?

46 Where next in your career?

My first head of department said that our first three years in teaching essentially follow this pattern:

- Year 1: learning through practice how to teach;
- Year 2: teaching with increased confidence;
- Year 3: teaching well and deciding whether to take on an additional responsibility.

Nowadays, in most schools, there is a more formal structure to help to give you a sense of how your career is progressing and whether you are building the skills and knowledge needed to become a more effective teacher. For example, there will be a milestone at the end of your first year, in which you will be assessed on whether you are meeting teacher standards.

A few years later, there may be some form of assessment to see whether you are continuing to develop and whether you are eligible for what is currently known as the upper pay spine – a different pay rate for teachers who have mastered the basics and are now in a position to make a wider contribution to the school, through coaching and training other colleagues.

Traditionally in schools, promotion has been about taking on responsibilities beyond the classroom. That has meant becoming a 'coordinator' of something or 'assistant' something or 'second in' something.

So, at some point, you are going to have to decide whether promotion into a leadership role is for you. It essentially means taking responsibility not only for the quality of your own teaching, but also for that of others – whether in a department or house or year group.

Many of us found that there is a different kind of satisfaction in such roles. There is a challenge that comes through advising, coaching, supporting and challenging the work of others. You get the benefit of feeling that you are making a wider contribution within the school community. You get to work with other colleagues, beyond those in your own department. You get an insight into the broader picture of how to improve schools and, in particular, how to maintain high standards across disparate classrooms.

Inevitably, however, what also comes with the territory of leadership is the need to have difficult conversations – to be prepared to challenge a colleague whose expectations and work may be causing concern to students, parents or colleagues.

To give you a flavour of whether taking on a responsibility might be for you, here is a list of the kinds of issue you might have to tackle as, say, second in department or deputy head of year. They are all situations I present as part of interviews for promoted posts.

Reading them will give you a sense of whether the step from the classroom – responsible for your own classes – to a leadership role – responsible now for other people's teaching and tutoring too – is for you. See what you think.

- During a routine planner check, you are informed that Teacher A doesn't appear to be setting homework. He happens to be a deputy or assistant headteacher. What do you do?

- Student B has a reputation for always getting into trouble. When you investigate, you find he is actually very good in certain lessons and terrible in others. The common factor in lessons where he does badly appears to be the attitude of the teacher. What do you do?

219

Next steps

- Your year team is aiming to introduce a new approach to recording extra-curricular contributions, which you believe will motivate students. At a tutor meeting, Teacher C has seen it all before and is publicly cynical. What do you do?

- You have looked at your team's exam results and you see a trend of underperformance with Teacher D. What do you do?

- A parent phones with concerns about behaviour in a particular class. She says that, in the last lesson, the teacher said to the whole class, 'You're all a waste of my time and I may as well not bother teaching you'. What do you do?

- You have three Year 11 classes to allocate to three members of staff (yourself, a new teacher to the school and a respected teacher who has been at the school for a number of years and who is very strict but gets moderate progress from students). The three classes are all very different – the first is very able and is likely to be a potential AS pool; the second has many C/D borderline students but quite challenging behaviour; the last is described as a 'lovely class who are always quiet'. What do you do?

- Students complain to you that Teacher E's lessons are deeply boring. You are aware that she never follows guidance on starters, plenaries, pace and variety. However, her results at GCSE and A level are impressive, and she intends to retire in three years. Should you do anything?

- A student tells a teacher that Teacher F has prodded him in the chest when telling him off. He says that another student witnessed it, and that the incident amounts to assault. A letter of complaint follows. What do you do?

- A parent says she will go the newspapers because the school refuses to allow her daughter to wear a nose stud. She says you are suppressing her human rights. What do you do?

How do you react to these 'management dilemmas'? Can you see yourself wanting to get involved in dealing with issues like these?

Promoted roles in schools are often accompanied by people talking of losing your own focus on teaching, being drawn away from the classroom, 'being on the greasy pole of management'.

What you are less likely to hear is that taking on responsibilities brings new satisfactions – for example, feeling that you are making a difference beyond your own classroom, helping a wider range of students, developing other teachers and colleagues and using a broader range of skills.

So, as you reach that point where you begin to debate with yourself where your next career step might take you, it is worth reflecting on your principles (what matters to you in education?), your resilience (can you deal with sometimes-unpleasant but often-necessary, difficult conversations?) and your own motivation.

Then, spend some time finding out about other people's roles – what does second in department do that is distinctive, for example? What is the day-to-day reality of being head of year? Spend some time talking to colleagues already in these roles; listen to them; try to spend some time observing them in parts of their job that are different from yours.

TALKING POINTS

- So, instinctively, what do you think?
- Do you find yourself drawn to the idea of a promoted role and wider responsibilities?
- If not, how do you see yourself continuing to develop as a teacher?

Afterword

So that's it: the end of more than 200 pages of advice, designed to take you from those fledgling thoughts of 'Is teaching for me?' to a growing sense that you are becoming a confident teacher thinking of how to develop your career.

I hope you have found the guidance useful, even where you have disagreed with its suggestions or been antagonised by the tone.

Here, as we part company, are my final three suggestions for how to make your career in teaching as enjoyable, unpredictable and endlessly stimulating as mine has been.

First, be a lifelong learner.

The best teachers are pretty obsessive about their subject. They are always reading, discussing and researching new ideas, new books and new approaches. They continue to do this into their retirement. Their subject is deep in their bloodstream: they almost literally can't live without it. Be like that.

Second, be realistic.

Teaching is a job. You will have good days and bad days. Colleagues will sometimes behave unpredictably, irrationally and irritatingly. So they will in other careers – but teaching has particular pressures. Accept this and, on your worst days, remember that it is a job: don't let small confrontations or disagreements keep you awake at night or, much worse, lead you into not talking to particular colleagues. If there is an issue, a difficult conversation to be had, some disputed air to be cleared, make it a priority to do that early on the next day. Don't let issues fester.

This applies even more with young people. Whatever the apparent sophistication of the world they inhabit, children are children. They are finding their way in life. They need us, as adults, to help to show them how to cope with life's uncertainties. They especially need us to help equip them with the skills and knowledge that will set them on their way. Keep enjoying working with young people, but remember that you are the adult, and that there will be times when you need to be forceful, sharp, boring or critical. They are students, not friends, and keeping those professional boundaries is fundamental to the job, especially amid the blurred boundaries of social media.

Thus, your students will sometimes disappoint you, sometimes let you down. The compensation is that, on other occasions, they will amaze and inspire you. Stay realistic, rather than letting yourself spiral into gloom after a bad lesson. Teaching, more than many jobs, has its own rhythms, its own psychological peaks and troughs. Learn to accept this. Learn that, even on your darkest days, with the most challenging class and the most disappointing lesson, it is just a job. Tomorrow is a new day.

Third, be self-aware.

Too many schools have, somewhere at the edge of the classroom or lurking in the online undergrowth of Twitter, the teachers who have become embittered and cynical.

If you find yourself disliking the job, if you are going through the motions, if you are seeing only the negative aspects of the job, if you find yourself increasingly socialising, in and out of school, with teachers who espouse a world-weary view, if it feels like everything is the management's fault, if you don't care about your planning, your marking, your teaching, then heed the signs.

You don't want to end up the wizened dinosaur of the staffroom, the teacher colleagues don't want to mix with and students would prefer not to be taught by.

Afterword

In other words, put bluntly, if you start to sense that you were wrong and that teaching isn't any longer the career for you, then act upon your instinct. Start seeking something new. Change careers.

Because teaching – if you are right for it – is a fabulous career. You get to work with interesting, educated, articulate people. You get to explore a subject you love. You get to see the way the ideas that caught your interest and imagination ignite the passions of the next generation. You get to do a job that endlessly surprises and gives the satisfaction of making an impact – occasionally a major impact – on your students.

Yes, teaching is a wonderful career. There – the secret is out. And I hope that you, like me, will have a really rewarding and enriching time, full of the optimism, earnestness and humour so often radiated by young people.

Welcome to teaching.

Geoff Barton
Suffolk, May 2014

Appendix A

Glossary of educational terms

As a profession, teaching is full of abbreviations, acronyms and jargon. Here, based on the glossary produced by the *Times Educational Supplement*, is a straightforward A–Z guide to some of the key terms you will need to know.

I am including these words because I think you need to know them, but definitely not because you ought to use them. In fact, especially when speaking and writing to students and parents, actively avoid using most of these terms, or at least spell abbreviations out in full, so that parents don't feel that we are simply using teacher jargon to confuse, befuddle or patronise them.

Academies

Academies are independent, state-funded schools. These schools have more freedom over their finances, the curriculum they teach and teachers' pay and conditions. They are funded directly by central government, rather than by the local authority.

ADD/ADHD

Attention Deficit Disorder: a condition whereby a child has a short concentration span and is unable to remain on task.

Admission authority

The official body responsible for rules offering school places, it also decides which children will be offered a place. For most schools, this is the governing body, but, for community and voluntary controlled schools, it is the local authority.

Admission criteria

These are the rules agreed by the admission authority to decide who will get school places.

AOTTs

Adults other than teachers: i.e. people who do not hold a recognised teaching qualification but who work in schools with the permission of the headteacher. Examples might include sports coaches and peripatetic music teachers.

Asperger syndrome

Asperger syndrome is an autistic spectrum disorder. The National Autistic Society says: 'People with Asperger syndrome find it more difficult to read the signals that most of us take for granted. As a result they find it more difficult to communicate and relate to others.'

Assessment for learning

Perhaps the simplest definition of this was given by Black and Wiliam in 1998, in 'Inside the black box' (in *Assessment in Education*): assessment for learning can be defined as 'all those activities undertaken by teachers and/or by their students which provide information to be used as feedback to modify the teaching and learning activities in which they are engaged'.

Autism

Autism is defined by the National Autistic Society as:

> A lifelong developmental disability that affects the way a person communicates and relates to others in a meaningful way ... people with autism can often have accompanying learning disabilities but everyone with the condition shares a difficulty in making sense of the world.

It involves problems with social interaction, social communication and imagination.

AWPU

Age-weighted pupil unit: the sum of money allocated to a school for each pupil, according to age. This is the basic unit of funding for the school.

BSL

British Sign Language is a language mainly used by deaf people. It uses hand shapes, facial expressions, lip patterns and upper-body and head movements.

Catchment area

An area served by a school, covering a number of roads or parts of roads. All houses in a borough and some outside the borough are in the catchment area of a school.

Cognitive ability tests

A set of tests for children between seven and fifteen years old. The tests include verbal reasoning, quantitative reasoning and non-verbal reasoning. They are often used in schools as additional evidence of a student's strengths and weaknesses, beyond narrow tests of academic ability.

Common entrance

This is the entrance exam for many independent senior schools, which can be sat at eleven, twelve or thirteen. The papers are set centrally, but marking is done by the school that the child is applying to attend.

Community school

A local authority-run county school, this is the standard type of maintained school. It is also a type of school that opens its facilities to local people outside lesson times.

Comprehensive school

This is a secondary school that takes all children living locally, without resorting to entrance exams, and educates them together.

Contact time

The hours teachers are timetabled to spend with pupils.

Core subjects

 These are compulsory subjects under the National Curriculum in England and Wales. The core subjects are currently under review, but, at the moment, children in state schools from ages eleven to fourteen study: English, Maths, Science, D&T, ICT, History, Geography, MFL, Art and Design, Music, Citizenship and PE. At KS4, the core subjects are Maths, English and Science. For more details on the compulsory subjects for each key stage, visit the school curriculum page of the government website (www.gov.uk/national-curriculum).

Cover supervisors

 These are suitably trained support staff who supervise pupils carrying out pre-prepared exercises when teaching staff are on short-term absence. For more on the day-to-day tasks, see: www. education.gov.uk/schools/careers/traininganddevelopment/staff/ b00202532/school-support-staff/roles/learning/cover-supervisor.

CPD

Continuing professional development: CPD includes any activity that increases teachers' knowledge or understanding and their effectiveness in schools. It can help raise teaching and learning standards and improve job satisfaction.

Daily act of collective worship

Assembly. All schools are supposed to do this. In practice, many secondary schools do not or cannot. By law, it is meant to be of a broadly Christian nature.

DfE

The Department for Education is responsible for education and children's services in England.

Differentiation

Differentiation is the term used to describe the way in which teaching methods and the curriculum are adapted to meet the individual learning needs of learners. Although the term differentiation is most frequently found in the context of students with learning difficulties and/or disabilities, differentiation applies to all teaching contexts: even where students have been placed in sets rather than a mixed-ability class, you will have students of different needs and abilities.

Dyscalculia

Dyscalculia affects the ability to acquire arithmetical skills. Sufferers may have difficulty understanding simple number concepts and often have problems learning number facts and procedures.

Dyslexia

 Dyslexia is a learning difficulty of which the chief manifestation is a particular difficulty with reading and spelling. For more information go to the British Dyslexia Association website (www.bdadyslexia.org.uk).

Dyspraxia

Dyspraxia is generally recognised as an impairment or immaturity of the organisation of movement. Associated with this may be problems of language, perception and thought.

EAL

English as an additional language: refers to children whose first language(s) is/are not English and who may not yet be speaking English fluently or even at all.

EBD

Emotional and behavioural difficulties: children who display these problems may be placed on the Special Needs Register and given extra support. See SEN.

English Baccalaureate

The English Baccalaureate is a performance measure introduced in the 2010 performance tables. It recognises the success of pupils who get GCSEs or IGCSEs at grades A*–C across a core of academic subjects – English, Maths, History or Geography, the sciences and a language.

EOTAS

Education other than at school, e.g. home education.

ESOL

English for speakers of other languages or English as a second or other language.

EWO

Education Welfare Officer: these people work with schools, pupils and families to find solutions to poor school attendance. They are also known as education social workers.

Exclusion, permanent

Being expelled, usually for bad behaviour.

Exclusion, temporary

Suspension for up to forty-five days a year.

Failing school

A school ruled by an Ofsted inspection team to be failing to give its pupils an acceptable standard of education.

Faith schools

Schools that are mainly run in the same way as other state schools; however, their faith status may be reflected in their religious education curriculum, admissions criteria and staffing policies.

Appendix A

Federation schools

A hard federation is an arrangement by which two or more schools share a single governing body. Federations can involve a mix of primary and secondary schools. Within the federation, each school retains its separate legal identity in respect of its budget, admissions and performance tables, and each is subject to a separate inspection by Ofsted.

FFT

The Fischer Family Trust is an educational charity that provides data that help schools to use pupil performance data more effectively.

Foundation Stage

Foundation Stage covers education provided from three years old through to the end of Reception year.

Free schools

Free schools are independent, state-funded schools that can be run by parents, teachers or other organisations or groups of people.

FSM

Free school meals: in the UK, children from poorer backgrounds tend to achieve less at all levels of education. Measuring which children are eligible for free school meals is one of the main ways in which schools and the government try to identify these students early on, in order to give them additional support and opportunities.

Functional skills

Functional skills are qualifications designed to help learners aged fourteen and older to build practical skills for work, education and everyday life. The skills cover English, maths and ICT.

GCSE

General Certificate of Education: academic examination of basic secondary education, generally taken by fourteen- to sixteen-year-olds, but available to anyone who would like to study a subject that interests them. GCSEs are available in a wide range of academic and work-related subjects. The government is currently in the process of revamping GCSEs.

Gifted and talented

The gifted are those with high ability in one or more academic subject, and the talented are those with high ability in sport, music, visual arts and/or performing arts. Schools are encouraged to identify the top 5–10 per cent of each year group as gifted or talented, regardless of the general level of ability within the school.

Grammar schools

These are maintained and independent schools that select all or most of their pupils by academic ability, usually with a test in Year 6.

HLTA

Higher-level teaching assistant.

HMCI

Her Majesty's Chief Inspector is statutorily responsible for Ofsted's inspection and regulatory work.

HMI

Her Majesty's Inspectorate: permanent inspection staff of Ofsted.

Home–school agreement

Home–school agreement contract is given to pupils and parents, outlining the aims and values of a school.

HOY

Head of year.

ICT

Information and Communication Technology: computer technology.

IEP

Individual Education Plan: identifies the special educational needs of a child and outlines targets and strategies to support their learning. It is usually completed by teacher in consultation with SEN co-ordinator.

ILO

Intended learning outcome: a concept used in some schools, ILOs describe what the students should be able to do or demonstrate, in terms of particular knowledge, skills and attitudes, by the end of a lesson.

Inclusion

Inclusion recognises the importance of catering for diverse needs. Inclusive principles highlight the importance of meeting children's individual needs.

Independent school

A school that is independent in its finances and governance – i.e. it is not dependent on national or local government for financing its operations and is instead funded by a combination of tuition charges, gifts and, in some cases, the investment yield of an endowment.

Induction year

The first year on the job for newly qualified teachers (NQTs), this is intended to be a continuation of training. A three-term period of assessment is usually completed in a single school year, providing NQTs with the tools they need to be successful teachers. NQTs can only begin induction when they have gained qualified teacher status (QTS).

INSET

In-service education and training: training for teachers that takes place during the school year.

Integration

Educating children with special educational needs together with children without special educational needs, in mainstream schools. See inclusion, which encompasses broader principles.

International Baccalaureate

Nowadays, the IB is a sixth-form course that students can opt to take instead of A levels. They have to study six subjects, three at standard level and three at advanced level. All students must study English, Maths and a foreign language, alongside three subjects of their own choosing.

ITT

Initial Teacher Training: Most people need to take an ITT course in order to gain QTS.

Junior school

For seven- to eleven-year-olds.

Key stages

The National Curriculum is organised into blocks of years called key stages. There are four key stages, as well as the Early Years Foundation Stage (EYFS).

- Key Stage 1: infants, five to seven years old;
- Key Stage 2: juniors, seven to eleven years old;
- Key Stage 3: lower secondary school, eleven to fourteen years old;
- Key Stage 4: GCSE, fourteen to sixteen years old.

LAC

Looked-after children: children who are in care or looked after by foster parents.

LDD

Learning difficulties and disabilities.

Local authority

Local government with responsibility for education (formerly known as local education authority).

LSA

Learning support assistant, also known as a teaching assistant: an assistant providing additional school support for pupils with special educational needs and/or disabilities.

Maintained schools

Publicly funded schools, usually including community schools, foundation schools, voluntary aided and controlled schools.

MFL

Modern Foreign Languages.

MLD

Moderate learning difficulties: a pupil with MLD will receive extra assistance under SEN provision. Pupils with MLD will have attainments well below expected levels in all or most areas of the curriculum.

National Curriculum

The National Curriculum outlines what children should be taught, from their first days in school to the onset of GCSE courses.

NATT

National Association of Teachers of Travellers: run by teachers working with travelling children.

NCB

National Children's Bureau: campaigns for children's rights.

NOR

Number on roll: the number of pupils registered at named school.

NPQH

National Professional Qualification for Headship. The now-optional qualification for headship.

NQT

Newly qualified teacher: a teacher in their first year of qualified teaching.

NVQ

National Vocational Qualification: a competence-based qualification, which means students learn practical, work-related tasks designed to help them develop the skills and knowledge to do a job effectively.

Ofqual

Ofqual regulates qualifications, examinations and assessments in England and vocational qualifications in Northern Ireland. Ofqual also regulates SATs, GCSEs, A levels, Diplomas and NVQs.

Ofsted

The Office for Standards in Education, Children's Services and Skills is an independent organisation that reports directly to Parliament.

PAN

Planned admissions number: the number of children the local authority (or governing body of an aided school) determines can be admitted to the school. Parents decide whether to appeal to any school to which they have applied and not been offered a place.

Pastoral support

Pastoral support programme (PSP): a school-based intervention to help individual pupils manage their behaviour. It is particularly necessary for those whose behaviour is deteriorating rapidly and who are in danger of permanent exclusion. The PSP should identify precise and realistic targets for the pupil to work towards. A nominated member of staff will oversee the PSP.

Pedagogy

The art of teaching.

Performance tables

Performance tables are published annually and list the results of a school's or college's performance based on national tests.

Personalised learning

The official definition of personalised learning is 'putting the learner at the heart of the education system'. The major components of personalised learning include: paying attention to every child's individual learning styles, motivations and needs; a rigorous use of pupil target setting linked to high-quality assessment; well-paced and enjoyable lessons; and pupils are supported by partnership with others well beyond the classroom.

Phonics

Phonics is a system of breaking down words into smaller components of sounds.

Plenary

A part of a lesson where the teacher reviews what's been learned, usually through questioning the pupils.

PPA

Planning, preparation and assessment time: teachers in state schools are guaranteed 10 per cent PPA time.

Preparatory school

Independent schools for young children, usually aged between five, eleven and thirteen, dedicated to preparing students for entry to independent, fee-paying secondary schools.

Professional skills tests

These are the tests that initial teacher training candidates need to pass before they can be recommended for QTS.

PRU

Pupil Referral Unit: established and maintained by an LA to provide education for pupils who would not otherwise receive suitable education because of exclusion or other reasons.

PSHE

Personal, Social and Health and Economic Education.

Pupil premium

Additional funding allocated to schools per free-school-meals pupil. Schools are able to decide how the pupil premium is spent.

QTLS

Qualified Teacher Learning and Skills is a teacher qualification in the learning and skills sector. It is equivalent to QTS.

QTS

A newly qualified teacher has qualified teacher status. This is the accreditation that allows a teacher to teach in state-maintained and special schools in England and Wales. To achieve QTS, the teacher must have completed a period of Initial Teacher Training (ITT).

RAISE

An abbreviation of RaiseOnline: reporting and analysis for improvement through school self-evaluation. These are the data provided to schools that help them evaluate the performance of their students.

Rarely cover

The National Agreement on Raising Standards and Tackling Workload, signed in January 2003, agreed that schools should create time for teachers to focus more on their teaching. One of the objectives was that teachers should only rarely cover for absent colleagues.

Appendix A

Roll

The number of pupils at the school.

SATs

Standard Attainment Tests (previously Standard Assessment Tasks) are now known as National Curriculum Tests. At KS2, the level will reflect the teacher's assessment and the national test results. The KS2 tests cover English, Maths and Science. At KS3, the level will be based on the teacher's assessment.

SDP

School Development Plan: a plan for what a school hopes to achieve within a prescribed time limit. It is used chiefly with governors to set the agenda for the school's improvement. Indeed, it is often called the 'school improvement plan'.

SEF

Self-evaluation form: the self-evaluation form helps schools to evaluate their own performance. The SEF is used by Ofsted inspectors before an inspection to help identify what to focus on. In many schools, departments and faculties will also develop an SEF.

SEN

Special Educational Needs: provision to support pupils with learning disabilities – may be provided through mainstream or more specialised education.

SENCO

Special Educational Needs Co-ordinator: this is the teacher responsible for ensuring that children with learning difficulties and emotional/behavioural problems receive appropriate support, overseeing the completion of IEPs and liaising with external agencies.

School Direct

School Direct replaced the Graduate Teacher Programme and was designed to enable schools to train graduates as teachers, in the skills and knowledge they need, in the way they want them trained.

Sixth form

Used to describe the final two years spent in secondary school. Students usually take A levels, but increasingly are also being offered more vocational qualifications such as GNVQs. There are also sixth form colleges, not tied to schools, which are much larger and offer a wider range of courses.

SLD

Severe learning difficulties: pupils with SLD will receive extra support under SEN provision, often attending a special school.

SLT/SMT

Senior Leadership Team/Senior Management Team: this usually consists of the headteacher, deputy head and other senior members of staff.

SMSC

 This cryptic acronym stands for spiritual, moral, social and cultural development in schools. Try the SMSC Online website (www.smsc. org.uk) for lesson advice and ideas.

SNS

Standard National Scale: pay scale for classroom teachers.

Special measures

According to the Schools Inspections Act of 1996, a school requiring special measures is one that is 'failing or likely to fail to give its pupils an acceptable standard of education'.

Special school

A special school provides education for children whose needs cannot be met in an ordinary school.

Statement

Pupils who are issued with a statement have a serious SEN requirement and will receive extra assistance with their learning. The statement sets out the child's needs and the help they should have. It is reviewed annually. See SEN.

STEM

Science, technology, engineering and maths subjects.

STRB

School Teachers' Review Body, established under the School Teachers' Pay and Conditions Act 1991 to report to the government on the statutory pay and conditions of school teachers in England and Wales.

Subject associations

 Subject associations are normally membership groups whose mission it is to further the teaching and learning of a specific subject in schools, colleges and universities. For more information visit the Council for Subject Associations website (www.subjectassociation. org.uk).

Supply teacher

Staff who provide cover for absent teachers.

TAs

 Teaching assistants: the role of a teaching assistant is varied, but will include some or all of the following: working one to one or with small groups of pupils; supporting pupils with learning difficulties or disabilities; preparing the classroom for lessons; tidying and keeping the classroom in order; creating displays and helping on school outings or events. Read more in our guide to becoming a teaching assistant (www.tes.co.uk/article.aspx?story Code=6167026).

Teaching schools

Teaching schools are a national network of schools that will play a leading role in the training and development of teachers, from ITT through to headship.

Teach First

Teach First is a charity that places and supports exceptional graduates teaching in challenging schools.

Appendix A

TEFL

Teaching English as a foreign language: the sort of teaching of English that happens in language schools. You can train to teach TEFL without being a trained 'teacher'. TEFL is not a qualification for teaching in mainstream schools.

Threshold

Performance threshold: crossing the threshold gives teachers access to the pay scale for post-threshold teachers (this is often called the upper pay scale). Individual applications are judged against a set of national performance standards set down by the DfE.

TLR

Teaching and Learning Responsibility: classroom teachers who take on extra responsibility could be awarded a TLR payment.

UCAS

UCAS is the organisation that handles university applications.

UTCs

University technical colleges are academies for fourteen- to nineteen-year-olds that focus on providing technical vocational education. They offer technical courses and work-related learning, combined with academic studies.

VLE

Virtual learning environment: a virtual classroom that allows teachers and students to communicate with each other online.

Voluntary aided schools

Voluntary aided schools are mainly religious or faith schools, although anyone can apply for a place. The governing body employs the staff and sets the admissions criteria. Schools' buildings and land are normally owned by a charitable foundation, often a religious organisation. The governing body contributes to building and maintenance costs.

Voluntary controlled schools

Voluntary controlled schools are local-authority maintained and they usually have a charitable religious foundation. The local authority is the admissions authority.

Appendix B
Subject word lists

As teachers, we model language all the time. We demonstrate to students how to use words, phrases and sentences that will enable them to think, speak, read and write like geographers and scientists.

Here are some of the 'power words' of different subjects. Have them on display. More importantly, use them, spell them out, repeat them and draw attention to them. In the process, you will be showing students how, as literate adults, we use language. You will draw them into the literacy club.

Art

abstract	easel	landscape
acrylic	exhibition	palette
charcoal	foreground	pastel
collage	frieze	perspective
collection	gallery	portrait
colour	highlight	sketch
crosshatch	illusion	spectrum
dimension	impasto	
display	kiln	

D&T

aesthetic
brief
carbohydrate
component
design
diet
disassemble
evaluation
fabric
fibre
flour
flowchart

hygiene
ingredient
innovation
knife/knives
linen
machine
manufacture
mineral
natural
nutrition
polyester
portfolio

presentation
production
protein
recipe
sew
specification
technology
tension
textile
vitamin

Drama

applause
character/
  characteristic
costume
curtain
director
dramatise
entrance
exit

freeze
improvise
inspire
lighting
movement
perform/
  performance
playwright
position

rehearse/rehearsal
role
scene/scenario
script
share
spotlight
stage
theatre/theatrical

English

advertise/
 advertisement
alliteration
apostrophe
atmosphere
chorus
clause
cliché
comma
comparison
conjunction
consonant
dialogue
exclamation

expression
figurative
genre
grammar
imagery
metaphor
myth
narrative/narrator
onomatopoeia
pamphlet
paragraph
personification
playwright
plural

prefix
preposition
resolution
rhyme
scene
simile
soliloquy
subordinate
suffix
synonym
tabloid
vocabulary
vowel

Geography

abroad
amenity
atlas
authority
climate
contour
country
county
desert
employment
erosion
estuary

function
globe
habitat
infrastructure
international
landscape
latitude
location
longitude
nation/national
physical
pollution

poverty
provision
region/regional
rural
settlement
situation
tourist/tourism
transport/
 transportation
urban
wealth
weather

History

agriculture/
  agricultural
bias
castle
cathedral
Catholic
chronology/
  chronological
citizen
civilisation
colony/colonisation
conflict
constitution/
  constitutional
contradict/

contradiction
current
defence
disease
document
dynasty
economy/economic/
  economical
emigration
government
immigrant
imperial/
  imperialism
independence
invasion

motive
parliament
politics/political
priest
propaganda
Protestant
rebel/rebellion
reign
religious
republic
revolt/revolution
siege
source
trade
traitor

ICT

binary
byte
cable
cartridge
CD-ROM
computer
connect/connection
cursor
data/database
delete
disk
document
electronic
graphic

hardware
icon
input
interactive
interface
Internet
justify
keyboard
megabyte
memory
modem
module
monitor
multimedia

network
output
password
preview
processor
program
scanner
sensor
server
software
spreadsheet
virus

Appendix B

Library

alphabet/
   alphabetical
anthology
article
author
catalogue
classification
content
copyright
dictionary
editor

encyclopaedia
extract
fantasy
genre
glossary
index
irrelevant/
   irrelevance
librarian
magazine
non-fiction

novel
photocopy
publisher
relevant/relevance
romance
section
series
system
thesaurus

Maths

addition
amount
angle
approximately
average
axis
calculate
centimetre
circumference
co-ordinate
decimal
degree
diameter
digit
divide/division
enough
equilateral

estimate
fraction
graph
guess
horizontal
isosceles
kilogram
litre
measure
metre
minus
multiply/
   multiplication
negative
parallel/
   parallelogram
perimeter

perpendicular
positive
quadrilateral
radius
regular
rhombus
rotate/rotation
square
subtraction
symmetry/
   symmetrical
triangle/triangular
vertical
volume
weight

Music

choir
chord
chromatic
composition/
   conductor
crotchet
dynamics
harmony
instrument/
   instrumental
interval
lyric

major
melody
minim
minor
musician
octave
orchestra/orchestral
ostinato
percussion
pitch
quaver
rhythm

scale
score
semibreve
synchronise
syncopation
tempo
ternary
timbre
triad
vocal

PE

active/activity
agile/agility
athlete/athletic
bicep
exercise
field
gym/gymnastic
hamstring

injury
league
medicine
mobile/mobility
muscle
personal
pitch
quadriceps

qualify
relay
squad
tactic
tournament
triceps

Appendix B

PSHE

able/ability
achieve/
  achievement
addict/addiction
approve/approval
communication
control
dependent/
  dependency
discipline

discussion
effort
emotion/emotional
encourage/
  encouragement
gender
generous/generosity
involve/involvement
prefer/preference
pressure

racism/racist
reality
relationship
represent/
  representative
reward
sanction
sexism/sexist
stereotype

RE

baptism
Bible/biblical
Buddhist/Buddhism
burial
celebrate/celebration
ceremony
Christian
commandment
commitment
creation
disciple
faith
festival
funeral

Hindu/Hinduism
hymn
immoral/immorality
Islam
Israel
Judaism/Jewish
marriage
miracle
moral/morality
Muslim
parable
pilgrim/pilgrimage
pray/prayer
prejudice

prophet
religion/religious
shrine
sign
Sikh/Sikhism
special
spirit/spiritual
symbol
synagogue
temple
wedding
worship

Science

absorb
acid
alkaline
amphibian
apparatus
chemical
circulate/circulation
combustion
condensation
cycle
digest/digestion
disperse/dispersal
dissolve
distil/distillation

element
evaporation
exchange
freeze
frequency
friction
function
growth
hazard
insect
laboratory
liquid
mammal
method

nutrient
organism
oxygen
particles
predator
reproduce
respire/respiration
solution
temperature
thermometer
vertebrate
vessel

What to read

You are a teacher. You should constantly be reading. This, I hope, goes without saying.

Just as the children who will turn into the most socially effective adults are those with an ingrained reading habit, so it is with teachers. Great teachers – even if not obsessive readers – are obsessive reflectors. They think endlessly about what they do and how they could do it better. And reading a lot helps us to do this.

So what are you reading?

During term time, you will endlessly and relentlessly read the work handed in by your students. This, however, doesn't count as real reading. You should routinely be reading blogs and reflections by teachers of your subject. You should be following people on Twitter who illuminate pedagogy and provide lesson ideas. You should be reading comments from people at subject conferences, or experts exploring the latest ideas. You should be keeping up with the way your subject is shifting at the boundaries of knowledge.

You should also, in your early days, be reading books about teaching. These might be autobiographical accounts or more formal guides to pedagogy. They might be books exploring the debate about skills versus knowledge.

If you are a teacher of History, you will want to keep abreast of the latest books on a period that especially interests you. If you are a teacher of Mathematics, you will want to read what people have written about why Maths matters and how we should teach it better. If you teach English, you will read weekly book reviews in newspapers and order far more books than you will manage, in reality, to read.

Whoever you are, you will read during term time.

When you get to holidays, you should be reading stuff too, but this time it is reading for pleasure – especially novels.

As you can tell, I read a lot. I have an upstairs book always on the go and a downstairs book and sometimes several others. The upstairs book is for relaxation. It may be a novel or an auto-biography, but it is usually something unrelated to teaching. The downstairs book will be work-related – a text about pedagogy or school leadership or an account of an education theory.

The more I read, the faster I read, and the more what I have read informs how I respond to what I read. Knowledge builds and informs what I do, the way I work, the stuff I teach.

So here are two lists: my five 'core' recommendations, each illustrating a slightly different aspect of educational writing, and then a similarly eclectic list of the education books I have most enjoyed.

Five essential books on education

- Ian Gilbert, *Essential Motivation* (Routledge, 2012):

  Ian is a remarkable conference speaker: see him if you can. He is funny, provocative and highly motivational. So is his book, which looks at how we can motivate young people in our classrooms.

- Doug Lemov, *Teach Like a Champion* (Wiley, 2010):

  This one comes with a DVD. I was sceptical about it at first – a compendium of forty-nine classroom techniques, from handing out books to explaining things clearly. Many of the approaches are illustrated through short video clips filmed in various US schools. Even if we find some of the methods stilted or formulaic, it is a brilliant resource for thinking about the essential skills required in teaching.

- Matthew Syed, *Bounce: The Myth of Talent and Practice* (Fourth Estate, 2011):

  There is a plethora of books about the nature of talent, learning and intelligence. I read lots of them, stealing ideas for my teaching and for assemblies. Syed's book is one of the best, because it is so well written, so readable. He uses neuroscience and sports motivation to explore the nature of top achievement.

- Mick Waters, *Thinking Aloud on Schooling* (Independent Thinking Press, 2013):

  This is a magisterial discussion on how schools are organised, how our country tests students and how we inspect. It is written with great verve and sets up a compelling argument for how we could be doing education differently.

- Malala Yousafzai and Christina Lamb, *I am Malala* (Weidenfeld & Nicolson, 2013):

  If ever there were a book to restore our perspective, to make us appreciate what we have and to remind us that, in some cultures, education is – quite literally – a matter of life or death, it is this autobiography by Malala Yousafzai, the extraordinary young woman who stood up to the Taliban. Read it if you have had a bad day.

Other recommendations:
- Phil Beadle, *How to Teach* (Crown House, 2010): funny, feisty and packed with hugely useful hints and ideas.
- Ron Berger, *An Ethic of Excellence* (Heinemann, 2003): a beautifully written and elegant slim volume that describes how to teach using a spirit of craftsmanship with students.

- David Brooks, *The Social Animal: A Story of How Success Happens* (Random House, 2011): fashionable and eminently readable book about how our life chances can be shaped by the right school and social environment.

- Daisy Christodoulou, *Seven Myths About Education* (Routledge, 2014): wilfully controversial and eminently readable, this book takes apart some of the myths about certain styles of teaching – for example, that teacher-led instruction is always passive.

- Guy Claxton, *What's the Point of School? Rediscovering the Heart of Education* (Oneworld, 2008): a wise reminder in an age of targets and tests of what real learning is about.

- Paul Ginnis, *The Teacher's Toolkit* (Crown House, 2002): a quirky and brilliantly practical collection of lesson activities to develop students' independence and increase their motivation.

- Malcolm Gladwell, *Blink* (Allen Lane, 2005): idiosyncratic, entertaining stuff on how first impressions (including by teachers) matter.

- Andy Griffith and Mark Burns, *Engaging Learners* (Osiris Education, 2012): packed with ideas designed to engage and motivate students and highly practical.

- John Hattie, *Visible Learning* (Routledge, 2009): a stunning compendium of what different education research tells us about which approaches are most effective in the classroom.

- E.D. Hirsch, *The Schools We Need and Why We Don't Have Them* (Anchor Books, 1996): on why knowledge is like Velcro and we should teach our pupils as much knowledge as possible: the more they know, the easier they will find it to learn.

- Oliver Quinlan, *Thinking Teacher* (independentthinkingpress, 2014): a manifesto for teachers who think deeply about their subject and encourage their students to do the same. It is a thought-provoking and entertaining read.

What to read

- Oliver Knight and David Benson, *Creating Outstanding Classrooms* (David Fulton, 2014): a comprehensive approach to consistent teaching across classrooms and departments, full of advice on teaching strategies and assessment.

- Michael Marland, *The Craft of the Classroom* (Heinemann, 1975): with his passion for teaching, his expertise in literacy and his extraordinary generosity, Marland remains a hero of mine, and this is the book that convinced me that I should become a teacher.

- Robert J. Marzano, *Building Background Knowledge for Academic Achievement* (ASCD, 2004): this does what he says: like Hirsch, he argues for more teaching of knowledge.

- Neil Mercer and Steve Hodgkinson, *Exploring Talk in School* (Sage, 2008): the most useful guide to using talk in the classroom. Superb.

- Graham Nuthall, *The Hidden Lives of Learners* (NZCER Press, 2007): an extraordinary account of detailed research into how students learn in classrooms, and how important it is that, as teachers, we are aware of their private worlds and experiences.

- Andrew Pollard, *Readings for Reflective Teaching* (Continuum, 2002): a comprehensive anthology of research papers on different aspects of classroom practice; excellent for enabling theory to inform our practice.

- Daniel Rigney, *The Matthew Effect: How Advantage Begets Further Advantage* (Columbia University Press, 2010): the concept at the core of this book has influenced me hugely: without really skilful teaching, the word-rich get richer and the word-poor get poorer. Great teachers redress the balance.

- Martin Robinson, *Trivium 21C* (Independentthinkingpress, 2013): a hugely learned and yet readable reaffirmation of the principles that matter most in education.

- Jim Smith, *The Lazy Teacher's Handbook* (Crown House, 2010): the title is slightly off-putting, but it is a great book for reassuring us that simple steps can help pupils to learn better.

- Paul Tough, *How Children Succeed* (Random House, 2012): uses the insights of psychology to explore the ways children learn and is especially robust on the need to accelerate the learning of children from disadvantaged backgrounds.

- Michael F.D. Young, *Bringing Knowledge Back In* (Routledge, 2008): the same theme: the link between knowledge and vocabulary and power.

Index

Index

Index